Charles "Lefty" Driesell

MERCER
UNIVERSITY PRESS

Endowed by
TOM WATSON BROWN
and
THE WATSON-BROWN FOUNDATION, INC.

Charles "Lefty" Driesell

A Basketball Legend

F. MARTIN HARMON

Mercer University Press | Macon, Georgia
35 Years of Publishing Excellence

MUP/ H893

Published by Mercer University Press, Macon, Georgia 31207
© 2014 by Mercer University Press
1400 Coleman Avenue
Macon, Georgia 31207
All rights reserved

9 8 7 6 5 4 3 2 1

Books published by Mercer University Press are printed on acid-free paper
that meets the requirements of the American National Standard for
Information Sciences—Permanence of Paper for Printed Library Materials.

ISBN   978-0-88146-506-8
Cataloging-in-Publication Data is available from the Library of Congress

Contents

Acknowledgments

After entering into an agreement to do this venture, my sincere thanks to my friends, "Lefty" and Joyce Driesell, for the hospitality they extended while hosting me in their home at Virginia Beach, Virginia for five days in November 2012. In addition, my appreciation to Coach Driesell for the access he provided to his files and the long hours he spent in sharing his many career stories, which now compose a major portion of this book. His interest and assistance made this all worthwhile.

Thanks also to the many friends, associates, and players of Coach Driesell who took part in interviews over a series of months in early 2013, patiently sharing their remembrances and accolades of "Lefty" throughout the chronological development of my manuscript. Along with "Lefty," they are the true storytellers contained within these pages. Without their valuable individual input, this very deserving recognition would not have been possible. I enjoyed each and every one and I thank them for their honesty and willingness to take part.

Additional thanks to Mike Holmes, assistant sports information director at Georgia State University, and the other SIDs he rallied in support of this project. Without the information Mike both provided and solicited, the hours needed to complete this work would have multiplied significantly and I am truly indebted for his timely support. Thanks also to the four colleges where Coach Driesell worked and their athletic communication personnel for the permission they all granted to use selected photographs from their archives.

And finally, thanks again to Mercer University Press for their initial interest and publication of this work, my second book under their esteemed supervision and support. Its production provides more than just the life history of one individual; it too is a sharing of college basketball history, especially in the South.

Special thanks also are in order for my wife, Sharon, who makes such projects possible at this advanced stage of our lives. Through her, I have the continued confidence and support to make such things happen as opportunities present themselves. With her I have been blessed and to her I am truly indebted.

Prologue

The Old Lefthander? It Was Worth a Try

It's not like it was the first time. It had definitely been done before. Jerry Tarkanian of UNLV fame had done it with Fresno State and so had Rollie Massimino, going from Villanova University and UNLV to Cleveland State. Weren't they famous, older coaches let go by major college programs…why not give it a try? Was it crazy to think someone who had built other programs before, turned losers to winners, might take on the challenge of turning around the losingest college basketball program in the country? After all, didn't "Lefty" Driesell have a daughter living in Atlanta?

As I sat there in a hotel room in Orlando, Florida, questions like these seemed to pop in and out of my head over and over. The Georgia State University women's basketball team had just completed its 1996–1997 season, eliminated earlier that night from the conference tournament and getting ready to head home the next day. Meanwhile, as I sat there, I was only an assistant athletic director for communications at the end of another basketball marathon. That's what the seasons are like for the worker bees called sports information directors, tireless people who promote the teams, manage the games, keep up with the stats, and provide a constant flow of information to the media on a daily basis for every team in the land. And despite the fact that my decade of tenure had earned a more exalted title by the time these big-time ideas were running rampant through my brain, an SID, in essence, was really all I was.

Once again, the Georgia State men's team would be in transition. Six years removed from its first and only NCAA Tournament berth in 1990–1991, hard times had returned to the Panthers, whose overall collegiate record at the time was 252–616. Soon the search for another head coach would pick up speed and there were sure to be candidates. A Division I head coaching job could always count on candidates regardless of the school. Soon, successful coaches at lower division schools or promising young assistant coaches from the Division I ranks would be testing the waters, making inquiries, evaluating the potential of a downtown school with a third-floor arena, but an enrollment of over 30,000. They would be aware of that "one shining moment" in 1990–1991 despite a barely winning record of 16–15. Wasn't that proof that lightening could strike, even at Georgia State? Without football to hog the limelight the way it did at most Southern universities, all it would take was the right person to turn things around on a permanent basis. As a new recruiting hot bed, wasn't Georgia high-school basketball getting better all the time? Somewhere there had to be the perfect young, enthusiastic, hardworking coach to make it happen—the perfect guy who, if given the chance, would finally put GSU basketball on the map before heading off to bigger and better things at one of the big-time schools in the power conferences.

But being a stepping-stone to bigger and better jobs would be okay as long as Georgia State got its share of success along the way, say consecutive winning seasons, which had never happened before. Why couldn't it still be the perfect proving ground for an up-and-comer in the Division I coaching ranks?

Those were the thoughts of a nearly 50-year-old SID accustomed to the mid-major ranks who had seen it all before. In other words, been there, done that...or here we go again.

Did I really want to see that cycle start over again? Maybe, over time, the new hire would prove the perfect choice, improve recruiting, but what if he didn't and how long would it take?

On the other hand, I had just seen it scroll across the television screen: "Lefty" Driesell let go at James Madison University. The guy who I remembered elevating tiny Davidson College to national prominence and the University of Maryland from ACC doormat to national power, the coach who people always seemed to question, especially after the Len Bias tragedy. I wondered…would he be interested in Georgia State? Would he consider at such an advanced stage of his career doing it one more time at perhaps the toughest place in the country? He had to be nearly 70. Would I be crazy asking such a question on the very day he was let go by another mid-major, one he had elevated before being shown the door—again?

I thought about the notoriety his selection would create. Here I was an SID at a downtown commuter school, a Division I program with only one NCAA Tournament appearance in 34 years of college basketball in the city of Atlanta, a major market, where focus was always on the pros, the University of Georgia, and Georgia Tech. But if I didn't ask, who would? Big-name coaches aren't in the habit of applying, but if they're available, why not? It wasn't like I had any confidence in the Georgia State administration to take advantage of the opportunity, and if we didn't, who would? What other Division I mid-major with similar designs on a big-name coach might be lurking out there at that very minute before swooping down to land Charles "Lefty" Driesell? What did waiting accomplish?

What was the name of that Virginia town where James Madison was located? Oh yeah, Harrisonburg. I wondered if he would ever have a listed number. Maybe it would be listed under Charles Driesell. After all, everybody knew him as "Lefty." Without the "Lefty," nobody would ever realize who that was. Maybe I would get lucky and they would have a Charles Driesell in the Harrisonburg phone book.

But lucky I wasn't. Information didn't have a Charles Driesell listed, only Chuck Driesell. I wondered…could that be his son? I knew he had one who was an assistant at James Madison. I took the number. It was worth a try—wasn't it?

Once again, I wondered about getting involved. The athletic director and the president, they were the ones whose job it was to select the next coach. But I also knew how long that would take and where it would probably lead. Wasn't it better to be proactive and go for it? And if he wasn't at all interested, at least I would have the satisfaction of knowing I tried—tried to move Georgia State Basketball to the front page for a change. After all, wasn't that my job…to generate as much publicity as possible, and what better way to generate publicity than if the lowly Panthers could get one of the winningest coaches ever? It was definitely worth a try.

With a deep breath, I placed the call. Yes, Chuck Driesell was his son and when I told him who I was and why I was calling, he surprised me by saying his father might be interested, but there was no way to know for sure until he called him. He said he would and I thanked him and left my return number there at the hotel. I figured that would probably be the end of it, but at least I had done my part—in the best interests of Georgia State University. Less than 30 minutes later the phone rang. It was "The Old Lefthander" himself with that unforgettable, gravelly voice that anyone who's ever heard it never forgets. "Martin," he said, as friendly and excited as if he had known me all his life. "This is 'Lefty' Driesell. Tell me about Georgia State." The rest, as they say, is history.

Please Note: This prologue is based on the actual initial approach and contact between the author and Charles "Lefty" Driesell, leading to his becoming head basketball coach at Georgia State University, March 1997.

"God knows I loved 'Lefty'…me and thousands of others who, on those cold winter nights in the early 1970s, would pack Cole (Field House) for one reason. To see 'Lefty.' Oh, we loved the young competitors he was developing and the tradition he was building, but we came to see 'Lefty.' He had charisma. You couldn't keep your eyes off him during warm-ups and then, we would wait for the big moment. The teams would go to the locker rooms five minutes before game time and then, with perfect timing, he would re-emerge stone-faced from the tunnel bolting to the bench. And just before he got there he would defiantly fling his arms triumphantly in the 'V' sign. The crowd went wild.

College basketball wasn't like it is these days. It was local, almost quaint. Certainly not as corporate as it is today, grooming pros for the NBA. So much has changed since those humble days and I submit that 'Lefty' Driesell was a big reason. He attracted so many fans. He invented Midnight Madness. People came for the show. It was grand to be a student at the University of Maryland. God bless you, 'Lefty' Driesell."

From a letter written by Jeff Rollins of Valencia, California, a 1971 University of Maryland graduate (published in the *Washington Post*, 24 February 2013).

1

Good Enough for One; Why Not the Other?

A Naismith Memorial Basketball Hall of Famer himself, Lute Olson, the retired former University of Iowa and Arizona head coach, once described Charles G. "Lefty" Driesell as "genuine"—as in, what you see is what you get. Olson made his characterization in a story for *Basketball Times* in March 2003.[1] A synonym for "genuine," according to *Roget's College Thesaurus*, is "legitimate."[2]

Another word that would be appropriate for the famously left-handed, foot-stomping denizen of NCAA Division I basketball sidelines for more than 40 years was "driven." Anyone who worked alongside "The Old Lefthander" at any of the four different colleges where he coached could honestly attest to as much. "My mother always told me there's no such word as 'can't,'" he repeatedly professed.[3]

Like a few other Division I head coaches of his era, the Jerry Tarkanians and Bobby Knights, his persona, at times, seemed too clearly defined for his own good. Certainly, opinions were made of him based on his showmanship, flamboyant sideline demeanor, and down-home, Southern style.[4] Also, like so many successful coaches, even in the present day, the label of having *never won the big one* was too often attached to his name, an acquired stigma based on his perceived abilities as a recruiter and prodigious acquirer of basketball talent (despite the fact he admittedly lost a lot more recruiting battles than he won).[5] Forget the fact that the majority of his career was spent toiling at the mid-major level, where success can realistically be measured only in conference championships and NCAA Tournament appearances, and the early part of his only opportunity in the "big-time," at the University of Maryland, came during the era when NCAA tourney berths were limited to only one team per league.[6]

Such rationalizations are not necessary. Instead, his record of 786 wins against only 394 losses speaks for itself. No coach wins nearly 70 percent of his games in any sport or at any level unless he can coach, and that's especially true of someone who turned around four losing programs. The first college basketball coach to win over 100 Division I games at four different places, "Lefty" could (and did) coach *with the best of 'em*. Prime examples include 22 seasons of 20 or more wins, 21 conference champions in four different leagues, ten First Team All-Americans, and ten Final Top Ten finishes.[7]

A nominee for hall of fame recognition since January 2000 and a finalist as early as 2003, Driesell's considerable coaching accomplishments did, justifiably, garner admission to the National Collegiate Basketball Hall of Fame in Kansas City, Missouri, in 2007. His was labeled the first class to go into that newly created shrine when really it was not. Instead, it was the first class after all the college coaches, players, and contributors already enshrined in the original and more recognized Naismith Memorial Hall of Fame in Springfield, Massachusetts, went in automatically—a total of 173 people, what was termed "the founding class."[8]

That list included a number of "Lefty's" coaching predecessors and contemporaries, who like him never won a Division I national championship and, with only one exception, never reached the NCAA Final Four. Among that group (with the year they were inducted) were Western Kentucky's Ed Diddle (1972), Washington's Marv Harshman (1985), Oregon

State's Ralph Miller (1988), St. John's Lou Carneseca (1992), Princeton's Pete Carril (1997), and Temple's John Chaney (2001), deserving inductees all, but certainly no more deserving than Driesell, who won more games than any of them.[9] The difference: all of them went in before the selectors for the original Naismith Hall in Springfield began making more concerted efforts to induct more retired professionals—players and coaches—women, foreign greats, referees, lower level coaching legends, and contributors such as commissioners, administrators, and other influential basketball ambassadors.[10] Between Chaney's class in 2002 and 2012, the only men's college coaches to achieve induction at Springfield were those with at least one Division I national title on their resume.[11]

In other words, the criteria for getting in have become much broader and tougher in the past decade. That's not to say the Chaneys, Diddles, Harshmans, Carnesecas, Carrils, and Millers were not deserving. They certainly were and still are, but based on their inclusion, so was (and is) "Lefty" Driesell, who has apparently been penalized for sticking around too long. Maybe if he had retired before his final coaching foray of five years at Georgia State University (1997–2002), Driesell could have gotten in with 103 fewer wins and 59 fewer losses. That still would have left him with more Division I wins (683) than all but Diddle from the previously mentioned group and nine more than the next closest (Miller with 674).

Or, if you believe the prevailing and often documented public perception of why "Lefty" is not in the Naismith Memorial Basketball Hall of Fame, maybe the broader pool of candidates is not so much to blame. Esteemed sportswriters like John Feinstein and David Elfin, both of whom have covered Beltway sports for years, obviously thought so when they authored columns eight years apart, 2003 and 2011, columns that exhumed the now famous tragedy that was Len Bias's death and the resulting mid-80s fallout at the University of Maryland. In them, both placed blame for the fact "Lefty" Driesell was not (and might never be) in the Naismith Memorial Basketball Hall of Fame squarely on the repercussions and stigma left over from that fateful drama.[12] Feinstein also mentioned the omission in a book and another article for the *Washington Post* in 2008, one in which he challenged Driesell's contemporaries already in the Hall to get behind his candidacy.[13] Closer to home, Virginia writers like Bob Molinaro and Dave Fairbank have long decried the Springfield absence of the Tidewater's favorite son, and columnist Jeff Schultz has repeatedly sounded the alarm at Driesell's final coaching stop, Atlanta.[14]

Such writings by area sports scribes have kept alive the concept of "Lefty" as scapegoat for all that happened on that fateful night after the 1986 NBA Draft and all the lives those events touched and changed. In the court of public opinion, it's certainly been easy to make that assumption, and because of a 2011 article in *USA Today* in which Jerry Colangelo, chairman of the Naismith Memorial Hall Board of Governors, was credited with stating he was willing to divulge what goes into the process and why someone was selected or not, it should be easier to confirm now.[15] Unfortunately, a request for just such a response in 2013 through Colangelo's assistant elicited no response.[16] As a result, Colangelo's previous confirmation to at least one known basketball insider (who for publication purposes will remain anonymous) that the bias created by the Bias tragedy does indeed continue to haunt Driesell's legacy, including any and all discussions of his candidacy for his sport's primary hall of fame, is really the only confirmation needed to assume as much.

Unlike others under recent consideration, Driesell has always maintained he was never guilty of National Collegiate Athletic Association violations at any of the four schools where he coached (a fact confirmed by Cameron Schuh of the NCAA Enforcement Division).[17] He claims not once was any kind of penalty or probation levied on Davidson, Maryland, James Madison, or Georgia State while on his watch. Yet, he's often been lumped with known NCAA rule-breakers like Tarkanian and Eddie Sutton (of Creighton, Arkansas, Kentucky, and Oklahoma State fame)[18] because one of his players, a full grown, 22-year-old, legally accountable adult male, tragically died because of his own bad decisions—decisions Driesell knew nothing about.

It's almost as if he's been placed in a separate category of rejection because of who his purported transgressions involved. Albeit, *"his player"* who died had the potential to be one of the greatest players ever—possibly even on the level of his collegiate contemporary, Michael Jordan,[19] generally recognized as the greatest—and such a loss was probably felt by the entire basketball community and fandom a lot more grievously than *a more human* casualty would have been. If, for instance, the player who died that night of a drug overdose had not been a two-time Atlantic Coast Conference All-American, the second pick in the NBA Draft by the Boston Celtics,[20] and even then one of the projected greats of all time, would the fallout have been even remotely as consuming? As crude and uncaring as it may sound, how much would the legacy of "Lefty" Driesell been tainted if a benchwarmer and not the great Len Bias had overdosed that night?

Even the Reverend Jesse Jackson, a candidate for United States President both before and after Bias's death who got famously involved at the funeral, was later quoted in C. Fraser

Smith's 1992 book, *Lenny, "Lefty," and the Chancellor*, for remarking at the time, "If we had lost another plant, a lesser flower, we would not be here, but God chose a rose, a rose of our generation."[21] That same book even noted that several weeks earlier a drunken coed had fallen to her death out of a UM dormitory window, but there had been no memorial service for her. In fact, "no one knew the young woman's name."[22]

Such questions, statements, and facts make it uncomfortable but nonetheless legitimate when looking back at the level of fallout from this one young man's unfortunate choice. In the wake of one person's accidental and tragic, but no less illegal, death, jobs were lost, reputations tarnished, and sports history was undoubtedly altered, as Dave Ungrady's *Born Ready—The Mixed Legacy of Len Bias* emphasized in 2011.[23] And more than any other person, all of the above applied to "Lefty" Driesell. How many more wins would he have had if he had not sat out the next two years not coaching? How many more wins would he have enjoyed and possible championships won if he had not had to leave the basketball hotbed he had helped develop at Maryland and in the greater D.C. area? And how much better would hoops history portray "Lefty" Driesell if not for the stupid, unlawful decision of another? Yet, despite all that, Len Bias has no greater defender—to this day—than Charles "Lefty" Driesell.[24]

As strange as it may seem, Driesell has much in common with the tainted heroes of other sports, stars saddled with one regrettable moment during otherwise standout careers—the Bill Buckners and Jackie Smiths of the sports world whose ball-between-the-legs error in the World Series and dropped touchdown pass in a Super Bowl will always be remembered first and foremost whenever their names resurface.[25] Unfortunately, the Bias incident will always be linked as an albatross to Driesell in much the same way.

Ironic, isn't it, that a great coach like Knight could have chair-throwing, player-choking, and press conference-humiliating incidents throughout his career that didn't keep him from getting into the Naismith Memorial Hall of Fame, all very personal malfunctions that didn't overshadow his obvious coaching accomplishments,[26] but Driesell has hypothetically (at least) been kept out by the misguided actions of another. While Chaney, the last of that previously discussed non-championship winning group to get in, once had a complete post-game press conference meltdown to the point of threatening the very life of his coaching adversary,[27] "Lefty" had no such outbursts for which he ever needed to apologize. The bottom line, at least so far, he's been good enough for the complimentary college hall of fame, but not the Naismith, the one named for basketball's founder.

Perhaps the documented statements of four of his coaching contemporaries who are in the Naismith Memorial Hall give proper expression to such confusing rationale:

University of North Carolina's Dean Smith (in 2004) – "I find it impossible to believe that "Lefty" Driesell isn't in the (Naismith) Basketball Hall of Fame. Look at the games he won at four different places. He should be in there."[28]

Duke University's Mike Krzyzewski (in 2003) – "'Lefty' is one of the top coaches ever in the college game. I think sometimes because a coach hasn't gone to the Final Four or won a national championship, people tend to diminish what they've accomplished. He put every ounce of effort into building programs that weren't successful before he got there. Not once did he take a program that was already thriving.

From Davidson to Maryland to James Madison to Georgia State, he built every one."[29]

Georgetown University's John Thompson (in 2012) – "'Lefty' has never been given the credit he deserves. The man was one of the best that ever did it and needs to be in the (Naismith) Hall of Fame."[30]

And, finally, the before mentioned Lute Olsen of the University of Arizona (in 2003)—"Unfortunately, somewhere along the line, I believe people lost sight of just how good a coach he was. I have always thought he never got the credit he deserved. Coach Driesell was an excellent recruiter, but he was also an excellent coach. He won over 100 games at four different schools. No one else had ever produced such a feat."[31]

Prior to his 2013 omission from the list of Naismith Memorial Finalists, Driesell admitted to Doug Roberson of the *Atlanta Journal/Constitution* that should he be selected, it would be "the greatest thing that happened to me in my basketball career."[32] Two weeks later, he told *Baltimore Sun* writer Jeff Barker, "It doesn't bother me that I'm not in there; I'd just like to know why."[33] At this writing, he was to remain on the nominee list through 2015. Meanwhile, three more Division I college coaches did get in as of 2013: UNLV's Tarkanian, Houston's 91-year-old Guy Lewis, and Louisville's still active Rick Pitino. All three had far less wins than Driesell (55 of Tarkanian's 784 had to be officially vacated due to NCAA violations), but all three had taken teams to multiple Final Fours and two had national titles.[34]

2

Norfolk's Best-Known Water Boy

"Driesell" is not a common name. It's certainly not a name found in most American phone books, and Charles Grice Driesell always wondered about his origins even before he became known as "Lefty." Always on the lookout for other Driesells during his travels as a college basketball coach, he never had much success when it came to uncovering extended branches of his family.

He did learn his grandfather, the first Frank Driesell, was an immigrant from what had been Austria-Hungary before the First World War, but he never knew much more than that about his family's roots.[35] Turns out his grandfather's family can be traced to Womelsdorf, Austria,[36] and upon coming to America, originally settled in Providence, Rhode Island. From there, the first Frank Driesell apparently turned some fortuitous skills as a jeweler into a job at Tiffany's in New York City before ultimately migrating down the Atlantic coast to Norfolk, Virginia. There he determined to open a jewelry store of his very own in 1883, F. Driesell & Son, and upon his death at age 70, ownership passed to "Lefty's" father, the second Frank Driesell.[37]

Thus was already well established the longest running jewelry store in Norfolk by the time "Lefty" was born on Christmas Day 1931. Although it was a family business, it was one he would show no interest in inheriting, especially after his family moved into a new, two-story house in a nice, tree-lined suburb just four blocks from Granby School. In those days,

Granby included grades 1–12. In fact, from second grade on, young Charles was allowed to walk to school. It was close enough that he could even tarry after the final bell on fall afternoons watching high school football practice, his first exposure to the world of athletics.[38]

Bill Story was the very successful head coach at Granby back then and he was always looking for volunteer help – at any age. Already established was the Granby tradition of younger boys assisting as team managers, the locally revered Granby Water Boys, so it wasn't surprising when he finally approached the obviously intrigued youngster, seen hanging around practice every day, about assisting his managerial crew.[39]

That was the beginning of a love affair with sports. Starting at age 10, Driesell would serve as a team manager for prep football and basketball throughout his elementary years, a team member in the truest sense who can be easily identified in old yearbooks or Norfolk newspaper clippings of the day due to his unusually youthful appearance. Regardless of the team or task, Driesell was as much a part of Granby athletics as the coaches and players, and gradually his presence on the sidelines made him a favorite of Granby fans. By the fourth grade, he was a letter winner. In fact, due to his constant presence at practice and/or games, his parents never had to worry much about his whereabouts and the legacy of Norfolk's most recognized water boy began to grow.[40]

It grew, in fact, to the point that once when a new teacher spotted the young Driesell naively striking matches outside on the brick walls of the school, she told him he would have to go see Coach Story for some much needed discipline if he thought such potentially destructive behavior could be tolerated. That's when Story came to his rescue, assuring her that young Charles was the last person they should ever again need to worry about, since the last thing he would purposely do was anything that might hurt Granby.[41]

According to his sister, Martha Radcliffe, who is just 18 months younger, "Lefty" was a "gym rat."

> There weren't many boys his age in our neighborhood, so "Lefty" would hang around with the older boys, especially the ones who played football and basketball. As early as I can remember, he was always interested in playing ball. In fact, when our parents needed to discipline him, the way they did it was take away his balls and bats, or whatever was in season at the time. That would bother him worse than anything. He used to sleep with a ball.[42]

Radcliffe also remembered the barefoot part of the waterboy legend as a team building thing. "'Lefty' would do anything if it was part of the Granby tradition," she said. "Anything the older boys started or encouraged, I'm sure he went along with. One of those guys gave him his nickname."[43]

Actually it was an older, Granby athletic star named Barney Gill, who Driesell credits with coining his now famous moniker. "Barney had a nickname for everybody," he recalled. "There was a bucktoothed guy he named 'Beaver' and a guy with big ears that he just called 'Ears.' At least being left-handed he didn't stick me with anything as bad as those."[44]

Along with his love and early entry into team sports, Driesell became equally known for his appetite. Radcliffe remembered a Christmas when their mother cooked two turkeys, "one just for 'Lefty' because he was always saying he didn't get enough to eat and always complaining about how his birthday was on Christmas and he didn't get to enjoy a separate, special day like most people." Always big for his age (nearly 12 pounds at birth), he grew up skinny, but not because he ever missed a meal—at least according to his sister.[45]

While sports was always his passion, Radcliffe pursued music, eventually majoring in it in college and teaching piano lessons while she was still in high school. "I used to practice the piano before going to school every morning, starting about 6 A.M., and I can remember he didn't like it one bit," she recalled. "He used to get up so mad because of my early practice, but I loved it every bit as much as he loved sports. When I was 16, our parents bought me a Baby Grand Piano and I still have it."[46]

One summer, when their father rented a beach house on Willoughby Spit, "Lefty" got his first paid job experience, working at Harrison's Boat House. He would arrive early to help get individual boats in the water and stay until sunset to help put them away. "They paid three dollars a day, sunup to sundown, $21 a week. It was good spending money back then for a guy too young to work anywhere else," he confirmed. Later he would work throughout high school at Edelblutes Service Station pumping gas, fixing tires, and learning as much as he could about automobiles. Located near Granby, it was a place where many of the school's athletes worked after school or on weekends, whenever they didn't have practice or games.[47]

After possibly the longest grade school managerial stint in history, Driesell finally began his own athletic playing career in ninth grade. He was determined to play everything—football, basketball, and baseball—and he did just that, becoming a fixture at end, forward, and first base for Granby teams throughout the late 1940s. Granby fielded great teams at that time with athletes like Chuck Stobbs, who would go on to pitch for the Boston Red Sox and Washington Senators; Hank Foiles, a catcher for the Pittsburgh Pirates; and the previously mentioned Barney Gill, who would star at running back for the University of Virginia and later serve as an assistant coach under gridiron great Earl Blaik at Army. "Lefty's" earliest basketball hero, however, played for another school. In fact, Driesell remembers Paul Gentry of John Marshall High School once scoring 50 points in a Virginia schoolboy game against Hopewell. Three years younger, Driesell wanted to emulate Gentry by "working on his game all summer," and to help with that goal, Granby Basketball Coach Donald Griffin got him a job painting the school locker rooms, a role that provided a key to the gym and access for four or five hours of practice every day between his sophomore and junior years.[48]

Such dedication paid off for Driesell as a junior, when he was runner-up for the city's outstanding player award; and as a senior, when he was named Norfolk's Most Outstanding Player, All-State, and MVP in the state tournament after leading Granby to a state championship. His concentration on basketball, however, didn't come until after starring in football as a freshman, when his goal of playing everything throughout high school was curtailed by an ear problem that required mastoid surgery, effectively eliminating his gridiron future. That same surgery would eventually resurface to haunt his collegiate basketball playing career at a place unwittingly determined by the future Mrs. "Lefty" Driesell.[49]

3

Education by Duke, Presentation by World Book

Joyce Driesell was already an important factor in "Lefty's" life by the time he made his college choice. A popular Granby cheerleader, who was one year behind her future husband in high school, she had already won his heart and influenced his future when he selected from among ten college basketball scholarship offers.

The University of Tennessee was his first choice. His previously mentioned high school hero, Paul Gentry, was already a basketball star with the Volunteers when Driesell narrowed his choice to UT, North Carolina State, and Duke University in Durham, North Carolina. His best friend, Dan Butler, a football star at Granby, was also being recruited by Tennessee and they had agreed to go to Knoxville and room together when a technicality emerged to change "Lefty's" mind. Turns out the legendary Tennessee football coach and athletic director at that time, General Robert Neyland, had instituted a rule prohibiting Vol athletes from being (or getting) married if they wished to retain their athletic eligibility, and with "Lefty" and Joyce already planning marriage sometime in the next two years, the Tennessee opportunity was suddenly not an option.[50]

"I just think Joyce told him, 'You go to Tennessee and you're going alone,'" Butler joked when reminded of Driesell's last-minute change of heart. "Sure I was disappointed when he didn't go to Tennessee with me as planned. I think he would have had a great career at Tennessee, but Joyce was always good for him, so I guess he made the right choice." A retired career Army veteran now living in Williamsburg, Virginia, Butler would go on to play on Neyland's 1951 national championship team.[51]

Meanwhile, married athletes were permitted at Duke, which had otherwise offered the same scholarship benefits as Tennessee. As strange as it now seems, football was king at Duke in those days with gridiron great Wallace Wade as coach. Blue Devil Basketball was just beginning to make a name for itself with Dick Groat as its first standout. Driesell credits Groat, a Collegiate Hall of Fame inductee the same year as "Lefty," with being the first player to use the jump shot as his primary offensive weapon.[52]

Actually, Groat believes he was just the first player to use the jump shot in the South. A native of Pittsburgh, Pennsylvania, where he would later star in Major League Baseball (shortstop) for his hometown Pirates, he first saw the jump shot being used at northern tournaments during visits home from school and decided to incorporate it into his own game when he returned to Duke. He stated,

> Everett Case at North Carolina State was the coach who really turned the South, and what became the Atlantic Coast Conference, onto basketball. He brought in a bunch of recruits from Indiana and forced everyone to start looking for better players up North. When I got to Duke, football was king, but we had a tremendous camaraderie within the whole athletic program and "Lefty" was part of that. He was two years behind me, but I always had tremendous respect for him.[53]

The proud owner of a special edition, 1933 Ford convertible (one reputedly originally owned by John D. Rockefeller) that he bought from a New York relative for $300, Driesell was not allowed to drive it to Duke his first year away from home due to freshman restrictions. As a result, he was always looking for ways to get home on holidays and weekends. On one such occasion, he posted a bulletin board notice at the university bookstore and was pleasantly surprised when another Norfolk-bound student offered him a ride. An older guy by the name of Jack Lucas, he was an ex-Marine who liked to drive fast. In fact, too fast for "Lefty's" taste. "Back then there was nothing but two-lane highways and the guy was doing about 100," Driesell recalled.

> When we stopped for a break, I told him I wanted to get out and hitch-hike the rest of the way, but he assured me he would slow down. Later I learned he had been the youngest Congressional Medal of Honor winner ever after falling on a grenade at Iwo Jima. He must have been the youngest because he lied about his age and stowed away on a troop ship. At least that's what he told me. After surviving the war and a bunch of surgeries (21 total), he also told me his nerves were shot, but he seemed like an okay guy.[54]

Less than a year later, before he and Joyce secretly tied the knot but after he was allowed to have his own car at Duke, he was guilty of his own lack of driving judgment when challenged to a race on his way back to Norfolk. He stated,

> I had forgotten to latch the hood after checking my oil before leaving Durham, and this guy pulled up beside me and said, "Hey buddy, will that thing go as fast as it looks?" When I said it would, he challenged me to a race and like a dummy, I accepted. But as soon as I got it going really fast, that big old hood flew up in my face and came completely off. It hit a tree and split in two. Of course, I stopped immediately and as he went by I will never forget him saying, "Hey buddy, you better get rid of that thing, it's falling apart."

Unable to find another, matching hood, "Lefty" always regretted eventually selling his convertible for $600. "I found a

1934 hood, but it never looked right and after we got married, Joyce kept telling me 'sell that thing, I'm tired of riding in that car,' so I finally sold it."[55] A 1933 Ford convertible is now worth about $64,000.[56]

After being restricted to the junior varsity, as all freshmen athletes were back then, Driesell began his sophomore year as a key reserve until his ear problems resurfaced. When it began draining, a member of the distinguished Duke Medical staff told him he would not be able to compete in Blue Devil sports again for fear of liability should a blow to his head cause him serious injury. At the same time, the surgeon who had originally performed the operation assured him and his family that such was not the case and he should be able to continue competition.

Meanwhile, the Duke physician maintained that during surgery they had removed a piece of Driesell's skull and that he might even be at risk of cerebral hemorrhage. Although allowed to retain his scholarship, that same doctor wanted "Lefty" barred from all Duke Sports, even intramurals. This tragic verdict, however, was more than "Lefty" was willing to accept and after sitting out one season, Duke Basketball Coach Harold Bradley quietly allowed him to play again as a junior and senior, although only in a backup role. By that time, they hoped no one would make an issue of the earlier Duke medical advice and "Lefty" was able to complete his final two years without further incident.[57]

Being relegated to substitute status has nevertheless gnawed at him ever since.

> Based on the way I was playing as a sophomore, I was about to become a fulltime starter and because of that one doctor's diagnosis, I've always had the belief that I was never allowed to attain as much as a player as I

otherwise could have. While I had other doctors saying that my prior surgery was not a concern, Bradley and the athletic administration had that in the back of their minds and my minutes were never the same, even as a senior.[58]

His high point as a college player came on a winning hook shot against North Carolina State during his final season, a newspaper clipping and photo of which remains one of his prized possessions.[59]

His junior year Duke finished 18–8, and his senior season the Blue Devils were 22–6 and ranked 10th nationally in the final polls. As a reserve, the 6–5 Driesell averaged 5.1 points per game and 2.1 rebounds. A Dean's List student, he also earned a Bachelor of Science Degree in education.[60]

But while "Lefty's" athletic ambitions were never fully realized at Duke, his personal plans were when he and Joyce eloped in the middle of his sophomore year. She was visiting him at Duke over the Christmas holidays and they didn't tell anyone about getting married by a justice of the peace in the Durham Hotel on 14 December 1951. She quietly returned home to Norfolk, where she worked as a secretary at the massive Naval Station Norfolk, the world's largest naval base. They didn't share the news with either of their families until June, when finally they could wait no longer in anticipation of reuniting in Durham as "Lefty's" junior year commenced that fall (50 years later they would be remarried in a church ceremony by their oldest daughter, Pamela, a Presbyterian minister). Although leaving her highly prized, federal civil service position at the naval base wasn't easy, Joyce was ready for the sacrifice and soon gainfully employed again in her new location at the Durham Blue Cross Blue Shield office.[61] "It paid the bills while 'Lefty' finished school and I enjoyed Durham very much—just like I've enjoyed every place we've lived through the years," she's admitted.[62]

Among the other big-name athletes at Duke during Driesell's time there was one Sonny Jurgensen, a future Pro Football Hall of Fame quarterback for the Washington Redskins whose path would cross "Lefty's" again in the D.C. area years later. Also there was a big, good-looking lineman by the name of Ed Meadows, who would go on to play for several National Football League teams. A legend for many reasons during his athletic career at Duke, much of which occurred away from the playing field, Meadows and Driesell roomed near each other during their first couple of years on campus. One of the craziest stories "Lefty" recalled from his time around "Big Ed" was when the 240-pounder asked to borrow a tie, pushed him into his closet, blocked the door, and proceeded to stuff newspaper into the crack at the bottom before setting it on fire. "I thought he was going to kill me," Driesell confessed, chuckling at the memory over 60 years later. "I could barely move and the smoke was getting thick before he finally opened the door. Ed laughed about it for weeks, but it wasn't funny at the time. He was a little crazy like that," Driesell remembered.[63]

Meanwhile, Driesell also recalled the benefits of knowing more responsible Duke personalities, including assistant basketball coach Tony Drago, someone he has felt a debt of gratitude to ever since. "Despite my ear problem, the doctor responsible for military examinations in Durham had me listed as draft eligible until Coach Drago, who he knew, convinced him otherwise. He got me a permanent 4F classification and kept me out of the Korean War," Driesell confessed.[64]

While in college, Driesell worked summers at Norfolk's Ford Motor Company Assembly Plant on the loading dock, which, according to him, was "really hard, physical work." At the same time, he was told that once he graduated from Duke, a better, easier, and higher paying job at the plant would be his for the asking and that turned out to be true upon his graduation in 1954. His new job was in Production Control, meaning he monitored how many cars of each model were produced every day on the main assembly line. "It was a boring job," he remembered. "I used to slip off to the bathroom and read the newspaper, but it paid $6,200 a year, which in those days was pretty good for someone just starting out."[65]

Boring, however, has never been something Driesell does very well and it didn't take long for him to begin looking at getting back into sports, the one thing he had always loved. Coaching became his goal and when Ray Casey, the athletic director at Granby, and Donald Griffin, a member of the school board, offered him their high school junior varsity position, he jumped at the chance even though it paid only $3,200, about half of what he was making at the Ford plant. He would coach Granby's JV football and basketball teams and teach history, but upon being told of the decision, Joyce was not happy. "I had to convince her that it was something I really wanted to do, something that had always been my dream," he maintained.[66]

It was also about that time that he read a book by legendary Kentucky Basketball Coach Adolph Rupp that prompted him to start bracketing his nickname with the now trademark quote marks whenever he signed anything. "In the book, Rupp made the statement that whenever he was asked for his autograph he would put quote marks on either side of his name so that people would know it wasn't a forgery," Driesell related. "That seemed smart to me, so I decided to do the same thing."[67]

Now in his 90s, Johnny Brown was on the coaching staff at Granby when Driesell started and remembered his earliest days. "I knew from the start he would make a good coach, because I had never seen anyone work as hard and invest as much time with individual players as he did," Brown said. "I used to kid him that he must have acquired his coaching ability through osmosis from all that water he passed out to the Granby teams growing up."[68]

In his first year of coaching, the Granby JV football team finished undefeated, and in his second they were undefeated and unscored upon. His basketball JV teams were Eastern District and city champions, and when Granby's head basketball coach left, he was promoted to the varsity position in 1957–1958 and finished 15–5 in his first crack at the Virginia high school varsity ranks. Obviously, coaching seemed to be the right fit for "Lefty" Driesell.[69] Meanwhile, in order to make up for his reduced pay (and keep Joyce happy), he acquired a job selling World Book Encyclopedias during his summer breaks at Granby. Little did he realize at the time that the things he learned while on that summer job would greatly assist him in his years ahead as a college basketball coach.

The first thing he did on his new job was acquire the addresses of all the Granby students. They and their parents formed his primary target audience. By personally going to their homes and introducing himself as the new Granby coach, he was able to gain admittance and immediate trust, and sell in the best interests of their children, the Granby students. "I presented World Book as an excellent way to help their son's or daughter's education," he said. "World Book provided a big, foldout presentation piece that I could take full advantage of by spreading it out on the floor or kitchen table for the whole family to see, and then talk my way through all the pictures and graphics. By the time I finished, there was no way most of them felt they could deny their child (or children) the advantages of owning World Book."

Utilizing the same dogged determination that would eventually characterize his coaching and recruiting style, Driesell sold more World Books than anyone else in the state of Virginia. He sold $25 and $32 sets as far away as Richmond. Later he would take the colorful foldout, printed presentation concept to new levels of salesmanship with his own recruiting creations, which, once again, were spread out in the family living room or kitchen so that everyone, the recruit, his siblings, his father, and especially his mother could get a good look at where their son was going and all the great opportunities that awaited once he got there. "Lefty" was (admittedly) an especially good salesman when it came to the mothers.[70]

Along with his early coaching duties and World Book sales, Driesell was able to continue his playing career by competing in semi-pro leagues throughout the Tidewater region. He acknowledged as much when he said, "I played in all the towns around there—against military teams and other teams with a lot of good players, many of whom were former college stars. I averaged about 37 points a game and once had 59. You can look it up. The (Minneapolis) Lakers even offered me a tryout. In those days the newspapers carried stories on all the local semi-pro leagues and I was pretty good."[71] He was also lucky when a teammate, Bill Chambers, the coach at Newport News High School (who still holds an amazing NCAA record of 51 rebounds in one game) was offered the head job at his alma mater, the College of William & Mary, the same nearby school from which "Lefty" would eventually earn a Master's Degree.

In fact, upon accepting the William & Mary job, Chambers immediately recommended "Lefty" for the suddenly vacant head coaching position at Newport News, a Virginia power. "They had a great tradition at Newport News," Driesell recalled. "Julie Conn, who had been a legendary coach there, was the athletic director and as much as I still loved Granby, I just felt I could be more successful at Newport News, so I took it even though I had four starters returning at Granby."[72] It was a momentous decision and opportunity, one that would ultimately put Driesell on the coaching fast-track.

4

57 Straight and College Bound

Still in his mid-20s at the time he moved from Granby to New-port News High School, "Lefty" Driesell left one good team and inherited another. The one he left behind had all of its starters returning except the state's leading scorer, Leo Anthony. The one he inherited was a state powerhouse in the midst of a 21-game winning streak when he took over for Coach Bill Chambers in 1957.[73]

It's now safe to say Anthony was Driesell's first star. The 6-foot guard, who would go on to a record-setting career at nearby Old Dominion University, where he still ranks as the Monarchs' No. 2 career scorer (despite only three years of varsity competition), averaged 23.6 points per game as a senior at Granby. His first recollection of "Lefty" as the new coach two years earlier was "when he obviously wanted to work on my passing," Anthony quipped. It seems the new coach was in the gym shooting when Anthony walked in and soon found himself "feeding" Driesell pass after pass for an hour or more. "I knew he had played at Duke and he turned out to be a great coach with a very disciplined approach," Anthony recalled. "He was also a very good player himself. While I was in high school, I saw a lot of his semi-pro games."[74]

In fact, when asked about his and Driesell's relationship at the time, Chambers recounted how they had really gotten to know each other while playing semi-pro together.

> My teams had won back-to-back state titles at Newport News when I got the offer to coach my alma mater,

William & Mary, and I had gotten to know "Lefty" while competing against Granby and playing with him in the semi-pro leagues. I remember one game where he caught an elbow at Fort Mead (near Petersburg) and lost consciousness. I spent the whole night with him at the Army Infirmary and got him back home the next day, so we had become pretty good buddies. I knew how hard he worked and how hard it was to beat his teams, so I recommended him to the Newport News principal. I've always been glad I did.[75]

The Typhoon, as Newport News was called, had won back-to-back state championships before he even got there and were led by one of the finest individual players Driesell ever coached, 6-foot, 3-inch Herman "Bucky" Keller. A four-time all-state selection, a rarity for any player in any state, Keller was what Driesell termed "a natural," who averaged 22 points per game as a senior when he was the state's player of the year for the third straight season while leading Newport News to an amazing three-year record of 75–2. The second leading career scorer in Virginia Group AAA history (1,808 points) at the time he graduated, Keller was a tough kid from an even tougher family life. According to Driesell, he had two older brothers who both served jail time, and Keller, who would average over 18 points a game during an outstanding college career at Virginia Tech, would later die young (38), reportedly from a stroke. Nevertheless, he would still make the Virginia Sports Hall of Fame in 1992 and the Lower Virginia Peninsula Hall of Fame in 2008—he was just that good.[76]

"Bucky was really good, but he couldn't tolerate trash talk. Once we were playing a team that kept trying to get in Bucky's head. One of their players was really picking at Bucky and all of a sudden he hauled off and punched the guy, bam—knocked him cold," Driesell recounted.

Well, after order was restored and Bucky was thrown out, I went up to him and said, "Bucky why did you do that?" He proceeds to tell me that he couldn't take it anymore. He had been asleep in the same room as one of his older brothers the night before when the police came to arrest him, so when this guy (the other player) started getting on his case with a lot of trash talk, he just couldn't take it. Thank goodness we won anyway.

In fact, Newport News didn't lose any that year, finishing 25–0 and winning a third straight state championship. Ironically, the team the Typhoon beat in the state finals was none other than Driesell's old Granby squad, 50–48. It marked the fourth time Newport News had played and defeated Granby that year, all very close games. "As every coach knows, it's hard enough to beat a team three times in one year, much less four, but that was a great high school team. With Bucky leading the way, those guys refused to lose," he said.[77]

Driesell's 25 wins on top of the 21 straight Newport News had when he got there gave the Typhoon 46 straight when the second of his three seasons there tipped off. They would go on to 11 more before losing, giving them a 57-game winning streak that still stands as the Virginia state high school record (more than the 51 straight won by Chesapeake Indian River High with future college and pro star Alonzo Mourning in the mid-1980s and the 54 straight won by the Moses Malone-led Petersburg High quintets of the early '70s). Nonetheless, the Typhoon's first loss in 58 games came with its share of controversy in a still famous game that took place in nearby Portsmouth against arch rival Woodrow Wilson High School. Indeed, the extremely heated game went to overtime and the score was tied when Woodrow Wilson got a shot at the buzzer that went in. The referees, however, were not sure if it came before or after the final horn.

In those days, the Virginia prep rule for such a situation called for them to turn the decision over to the official scorer, a less than objective method for deciding the final outcome when nearly all official scorers are appointed by, paid by, or (in many cases) even a member of the home school's staff. Such was the case that night and predictably the official scorer, a Woodrow Wilson teacher, ruled the basket was good. Pandemonium ensued and Driesell spent several minutes just getting his team safely off the court and into the locker room. By that time, the Portsmouth crowd was so exuberant the upper level bleachers collapsed, sending numerous spectators to the hospital that night. In recalling the scene, Driesell said, "I will never forget, as we were leaving they were carrying people out of there on stretchers and putting them into ambulances, but I didn't find out about the bleachers collapsing until later. I just figured there must have been a big fight among the fans after that controversial finish."

Never one to adhere to only one coaching style without considering his available talent and making adjustments from one year to the next, Driesell inherited a group of underhanded free-throw shooters when he got to Newport News and although he had always used and believed in the overhand style, it was not something he tried to change. "For the most part, they were all good at the underhanded style and shot about 80 percent. Why would I want to change them? I've always felt adapting was an important part of coaching and you don't mess with what works," he stressed.[78]

By the time Driesell's fifth year of high school varsity coaching (two at Granby, three at Newport News) reached a conclusion, his overall prep record was a gaudy 97–15, and despite being only 28 years old, his success was generating interest from the college ranks. Eddie Cameron, the athletic director at Duke whom the now famous Cameron Indoor Stadium is named for, was even interested in adding the young, former Blue Devil to his basketball coaching staff, but then head coach Vic Bubbas opted instead for North Carolina State product Bucky Waters.

That's why when the Davidson College head job opened up, Cameron was only too happy to help "Lefty" land that post at the cross state, all-male school near Charlotte, North Carolina.

> I took a pay cut of $200 ($6,200 to $6,000) to go from Newport News High School to Davidson College, but once again I convinced Joyce it was what I wanted to do. Nobody else wanted that job. Davidson was a Presbyterian school with 900 boys and no girls, but it was a college head job and it was Division I. They were 5–19 the year before I got there and hadn't had a winning season in 11 years. There was nowhere to go but up and that's where we were headed—up,

he proudly announced while thinking back. "I owed a great deal to my players and the two high schools where I coached, but the opportunity to coach college basketball was something I had always dreamed about and I was confident I could turn things around at Davidson. I had a plan. I was basically going to outwork everybody and that's what I did."[79]

5

Outworking Everybody at Davidson

Hired to replace outgoing coach Tom Scott, who remained as athletic director, the selection of "Lefty" Driesell is still remembered in Davidson College basketball media guides as one of the best "executive decisions" ever.[80] Although little known nationally after only coaching high school and despite being only 28 years of age, Driesell arrived at Davidson on "a mission" and knew he would have to hit the road and recruit players who could compete at the highest level of college basketball while meeting rigorous academic standards at the same time.

"Recruiting is selling and all coaching is more selling than teaching. Some coaches teach too much." he has always said. "You've got to sell your players on the school and your program, and then you've got to keep selling them on your philosophy."[81]

At Davidson, he would start selling right away. In his first season (1960–1961) with Scott's leftover players, the Wildcats would finish only 9–14, but in his first game as coach they gave a portent of things to come when they upset a nationally ranked Wake Forest team led by All-ACC guard Billy Packer, the same Billy Packer who would become one of the nation's premier college basketball television analysts in the years ahead. A true hoops historian and never one to forget a key basketball moment, Packer has never forgotten how his Demon Deacons were surprised by "little Davidson" and its new coach. When asked about it, he rationalized,

Well, you've got to understand; we didn't have our full complement of players that day, including our All-American, Len Chappell (due to injury). In fact, we had just added a couple of guys off the football team and in those days Davidson wasn't really considered a threat to us. At the same time, I had heard about "Lefty" Driesell from Bucky Keller, who was recruited by Wake at the same time I was and I don't want to take anything away from what they did that day. Bucky was right—they were well coached and really motivated.

It was the first of many times Driesell and Packer would cross paths during their basketball careers, including Packer's first TV game at North Carolina State (a Maryland win for Driesell in 1972). After the Davidson loss, that same Wake Forest team would go on to win two straight Atlantic Coast Conference championships, and Packer would go on to call Driesell "the greatest program builder ever in college basketball."[82]

D. G. Martin, a player on "Lefty's" first two Davidson teams and son of then school president Grier Martin, had his own take on that game and Driesell's first year at the helm. He said,

> That Wake Forest game really put us on the map. I think it validated "Lefty" as our coach and gave him the credibility and notice he needed to go out and bring in better players for our program. His coming was all very positive. I can remember how his practices were well organized and scripted, and we liked knowing how well prepared he was. He came with a prepared notebook, almost a textbook for what became Davidson basketball. We had never had anything like that. He looked at what was going on in other places and brought in things like weight training, which we had never done before.

Martin also remembered how his father had been confident about the hire even though Driesell was only 28.

> After the decision was made for Tom Scott to give up the head basketball duties, I can remember my father telling me they were "bringing in an exciting new coach, who had enjoyed incredible success at the high school level." A lot of people were questioning how young he was and if he just planned on using Davidson as a stepping stone, but my father had asked him about that and "Lefty" had said the only job he couldn't turn down if it was ever offered was Duke, where he had played and gone to school, and I think my Dad appreciated his honesty and the fact he didn't beat around the bush with an answer. "Lefty" was like that. He was a salesman, but he was never dishonest and having been a pretty good basketball player himself, I think my father had a really good feeling about him and their relationship got off to a great start."[83]

Driesell's first college recruit at Davidson was Terry Holland, a 6-foot, 7-inch forward from Clinton, North Carolina, who was also being recruited by Wake Forest. Although determined to target better players in order to elevate Davidson's performance, he knew that only good students could meet the school's lofty entrance requirements, effectively narrowing his list of potential recruits before he even started. "At Davidson, we recruited 100 players a year (all of whom were academically qualified) with the idea we could outwork everybody to land five or six," Driesell confirmed.

With a then all-male student body, Davidson was hardly a place to attract great players unless academics and one's future after basketball were uppermost in their college choice. By combining this prerequisite, however, with Driesell's desire to succeed, coaching, and tireless work ethic, Wildcat recruiting became prioritized in such a way that there was no wasted time or effort—he really couldn't afford any. With an annual recruiting budget of only $500 when he started, the recruits who also happened to be the best students were painstakingly identified and sought after without the obvious advantages of the big-time programs he was pitted against for their services.[84]

Holland still considers Driesell a great salesman as well as coach, who promised his mother that Davidson would become a Top 10 program and then backed it up. "After all, a great salesman has to be willing to overpromise and then figure a way to deliver on what he promised," Holland stated.

> "Lefty" sure did go out on a big limb that night when he overpromised my mother that if I came to Davidson, we would be in the Top 10, just like Wake Forest. At the time it seemed fortunate that I had to leave to take my girlfriend (eventually his wife) to the prom, but when I got home that night my mother had forged my signature on the Davidson admission form. I later joked that if "Lefty" had any lightning rods, he would have sold her some of those as well. The crazy end to that story is that by my senior year, he had Davidson ranked as high as third in the country. I was amazed, but my mother just said, "well, he told us that would happen."[85]

Utilizing an old, green athletic department Chevrolet station wagon with a mattress in the back so he could sleep in the car and avoid paying for motels, Driesell did, indeed, sell his program any way he could. With a gun that had belonged to his father underneath his pillow at night in case he needed to scare off attempted intruders (even though it didn't work), he would park next to service stations that provided available wash rooms when they opened the next morning. When he did stay in motels, they were always the cheapest he could find and sometimes so bad that dressers were moved against the door for added security.

When he signed Fred Hetzel of Washington, D.C., his first big-name recruit at Davidson a couple of years later, he was so excited in the moment that he invited the entire Hetzel family out to eat at one of Washington's finest restaurants. The only problem: when the bill came he didn't have enough cash on hand to cover the total and had to resort to asking Mr. Hetzel, Fred's father, if he could help on the bill with "Lefty's" promise of paying him back. "I was always having to go back to Dr. Martin to try and get more money to go after one player or another, and to his credit, he would always find a way to make it happen," Driesell remembered.[86]

Hetzel, a 6-foot, 8-inch center who earned All-American honors three times and was the first player taken in the 1965 NBA Draft by the San Francisco Warriors, undoubtedly had as much to do with Davidson's legendary rise from Southern Conference also-ran to nationally ranked power and "Lefty's" emerging reputation as a coach and program builder as any player. Like Holland, however, it was Hetzel's mother who may have sealed the deal in her son's recruitment.

> They had a pet snake and when I visited their home in Washington, I would let the snake crawl all over me. His mother said I was the only coach willing to do that. When "Whack" Hyder of Georgia Tech visited, she said that when he saw the snake the first time, he told her that where he came from they stomp on those kind of things. I think she really started to like me right then and there,

Driesell amusedly recalled.[87]

Another Driesell cost-cutting measure in those early days in an effort to stay within budget was to use strategically placed, passionate, and well-positioned Davidson alumni as a support mechanism for his recruiting travels. An example was Dr. Robert McCloud, a former Davidson player and graduate living in basketball rich Kentucky. "Lefty" would fly to the Bluegrass State and then use Dr. McCloud's car (and gas) to travel throughout the area visiting recruits.[88] Along with Hetzel, his out-of-state recruits encompassed some of the best-loved and hardest-working players in Davidson basketball history, including Jerry Cole from Texas, Don Davidson and Dick Snyder from Ohio, and Barry Teague from the before mentioned Kentucky (Madisonville).[89]

Teague, who was from a basketball-saturated area near the Kentucky-Indiana border, was recruited to play baseball at the University of Kentucky with the option of trying out for basketball as well under legendary coach Adolph Rupp. The fact the "Baron of the Bluegrass" had already signed another point guard against whom Teague had enjoyed a lot of success left a sour taste in his mouth, however, and he told personal friend and former Kentucky All-American Frank Ramsey that if he wasn't good enough to be recruited for the sport he wanted to play, he would rather play somewhere else. That place ended up being Davidson College, thanks to his future wife's brother, who was assistant director of admissions at Davidson. "My first impression of 'Lefty' was as a great salesman and promoter as well as coach," Teague said.

> Basically he just outworked people and he had a setup on campus where faculty and staff could bring in newspaper clippings to help him learn about good high school players in other places. My wife and I were already dating at the time, so her brother takes in a clipping about me as a player and the next thing you know, "Lefty" is recruiting me and my mother, as he did most guys, and I was going to Davidson.[90]

Along with recruiting, Driesell didn't leave many things to chance when it came to games either. One such moment came when Teague, who was instrumental in the team's overall success as a good ball-handling point guard from 1962 through 1965, developed a bad case of the flu with a high fever and, like all sick students in those days, was sent to the campus infirmary.

"The director of the infirmary was an older gentleman and he called to inform me that Barry would be unable to make our trip the next day to play the University of Richmond," Driesell reminisced.

> Well, we were nationally ranked and I needed Teague if at all possible to have a chance at Richmond, so I called the infirmary back and said I needed to check and see if there's any way if he felt better that we could take him with us and make a game-time decision on whether or not he was well enough to play. They proceeded to tell me that was out of the question because school policy required a student to remain in the infirmary until at least 24 hours had passed after their fever broke. I was like, you got to be kidding me, he's my point guard and you're telling me he can't play, so I called Barry that night and asked how he was feeling and he told me "coach I'm fine and I want to play," so I cooked up this idea where we would stop the team bus in front of the infirmary on our way out of town, open the door, and if he could, he would run out, jump on, and we would get out of town before he was missed. Unfortunately, they saw him leaving and yelled for him to stop, but we took off anyway. Well, being from Virginia, I knew a doctor who lived in Richmond and I had him come to the arena and check Barry out before the game, at halftime, and at the end. He played and played well, and we won by three points, 52–49. When I got back, I had a letter of reprimand from the dean of students. Barry's mother wasn't too happy either, but at least we won.[91]

And winning was something they did a lot of in those days. After the 14–11 mark in Driesell's second season at the helm, the Wildcats fashioned four straight seasons of 20 or more wins, going 20–7, 22–4, 24–2, and 21–7, respectively, between 1962 and 1966. The unprecedented success (Davidson had never enjoyed 20 wins before), coming as it did with such things as national rankings, three Southern Conference Tournament championships, and three NCAA Tournament berths created a never before experienced surge of basketball interest at the school, leading to home games with the likes of ACC powers Duke, North Carolina State, and Wake Forest, and the move of such games to the 11,000-seat Charlotte Coliseum.[92]

It was during that initial stretch of success that "Lefty" remembered offering Duke head coach Vic Bubas a $10,000 guarantee or 50 percent of the gate, whichever was greater, to play the Wildcats in Charlotte. "I made the offer after they had beaten us over there two straight years and he turned me down, so I called him yellow in the newspapers," Driesell stated. "That must have gotten his attention because they did finally play us in Charlotte and we won, 72–69, even though they had two All-Americans in Art Heyman and Jeff Mullins. That was the start of us leading the nation in attendance."[93] It was also the start of the Hetzel era at Davidson.

Hetzel was the school's career leader in both points and rebounds until Mike Maloy supplanted him in the latter category as the leader of Driesell's second group of Davidson standouts in the late 1960s. He was also eventually overtaken by more recent Wildcat stars in the scoring column. They surpassed his career point totals in four years after the advent of freshman eligibility (Hetzel having played only three at the varsity level). Nevertheless, he's still second and third, respectively, in rebounding and scoring,[94] and still amazed when he thinks back to the program he helped "Lefty" build.

He said,

There's no doubt they broke the mold when they made "Lefty" Driesell. What he did at Davidson is just as remarkable now as it was then. He built that program on a shoe string. He literally didn't have enough money to stay in a motel when he was recruiting me. I can remember one time his car got broken into and all his clothes stolen, but the next week he was back and just as determined as ever. I attended an all-boys high school, so going to Davidson wasn't that different for me, but that doesn't make it any less remarkable that he was able to recruit other, good players. It's really a testament to how great a salesman he was. He developed a great relationship with both of my parents and he never let up, beginning my sophomore year. I still don't know how he did it relative to his own family, but he did and no matter what he did later at Maryland, James Madison, and Georgia State, what he was able to do at Davidson will never be repeated.[95]

Hetzel, a great shooter, would play six seasons in the NBA after totaling 2,032 points at Davidson in 79 games, a phenomenal 25.7 career average. Twice he would score over 45 points in a single game, including a career high 53 versus Furman on 8 December 1964. Equally impressive was his 14.8 per game rebound average, all of which didn't just come against Southern Conference competition, but against nationally ranked teams like Duke, Wake Forest, and Ohio State. "That's another great thing 'Lefty' did," Hetzel pointed out. "He would always get us games out of conference against top-ranked teams."[96]

In addition to six non-conference meetings with Duke during Driesell's tenure, the Wildcats would play the likes of Syracuse, Michigan, and two-time national champion Cincinnati (1962) on a fairly regular basis, as well as many championship meetings with a then bitter Southern Conference rival, the University of West Virginia. They would also go 6–3 in games against Wake Forest, developing a good rivalry with the in-state Deacons and their wily coach "Bones" McKinney.[97] Driesell remembered one such early season encounter at Wake and McKinney's desire to use a promotional trick to spur attendance:

> So we're supposed to go to go over there later that week and Bones calls me and says, "Hey 'Lefty,' we need to do something to jack up attendance. Why don't I say something bad in the papers about you and after it comes out, you say something bad about me. That will get the fans fired up and ensure a good crowd." So that's what we did. He came out with something about how my team and coaching wasn't very good, and I came back about how much we were looking forward to going over there and teaching him a lesson. It worked because if memory serves it was close to a full house.[98]

In 1963–1964, the Wildcats also went to Ohio State, then in the midst of a 50-game home court winning streak following the Jerry Lucas and John Havlicek-led Buckeyes' run of three straight national championship appearances,[99] and came away with a shocking 94–73 victory en route to their first Final Top 10 ranking. Ohio natives Davidson and Snyder played great and afterwards legendary Ohio State Coach Fred Taylor accused Driesell of stealing both even though their home-state Buckeyes had never recruited either. "We added what I call the wheel offense for Ohio State," Driesell recalled. "I took my two post men, usually Holland and Hetzel, and had them set a double pick on the side with Snyder, who reversed the ball to the other side and looked for a return pass coming off the double screen. After they finally figured out how to stop that, Hetzel would just pop out and hit an open jumper. It screwed them up bad."[100] In fact, in a year in which they only lost at No. 3 Duke (with its renowned home court advantage) by seven points , 85–78, Davidson finished 10th in the nation and ahead of such established powers of the time as Bradley, Drake, Providence, San Francisco, Texas Western, Vanderbilt, North Carolina, and…Ohio State.[101]

Along with Hetzel, the other obvious star in Davidson's rise was Snyder, a good enough student to add Academic All-American status to his impressive list of college accomplishments. In fact, he was good enough as an all-around athlete coming out of high school to be recruited as a quarterback by Ohio State and Notre Dame.[102] Why he chose Davidson basketball over Notre Dame football is a legitimate question and one Teague, still a good friend, answered by saying,

> To this day, Dick Snyder is one of the greatest natural athletes I've ever seen. He could have been a pro in football, baseball, or whatever, but he wanted to play basketball and I think Davidson was the only school that recruited him for basketball. In fact, I think "Lefty" recruited him sight-unseen and just based on what people had told him about his athletic prowess. He could throw a football 70 yards, punt it 70 yards, and probably would have made a great college quarterback.[103]

Perhaps Driesell summed up Snyder's recruitment best when he shared this comment by his star years later: "Everybody knew I could be a good football player, but a lot of people didn't believe I could be a good college basketball player and I wanted to prove them wrong."[104]

A year behind Hetzel in school, Snyder was a slashing 6-foot 5-inch wingman in Driesell's double post, one guard offense. Following Hetzel's rather large footprints, he would earn Southern Conference Player-of-the-Year status and All-American honors on the court as well as the classroom by the time he was a senior, finishing with a 21.2 point average for his entire three-year varsity career. In fact, with Hetzel by then in the pros, he posted an impressive 26.2 average his senior year (1965–1966), including a career best 46 against Ohio University, a 96–63 rout. He would play 13 years in the NBA for the then St. Louis Hawks, Cleveland Cavaliers, Phoenix Suns, and Seattle Supersonics, and score over 10,000 points.[105]

Davidson, a very physical 6-foot, 5-inch, 210-pound defensive stalwart, manned the other wing while Holland patrolled the post opposite Hetzel during the 1963–1964 season, rounding out a starting five along with Teague at the point and Snyder that was probably the Wildcats' best in the early 1960s. Bill Jarman, an undersized but talented 6-foot, 5-inch center/forward from nearby Gastonia, North Carolina, was another of Driesell's earliest college stars. "I don't ever remember being taken out to rest," Teague stated. "As a starter for 'Lefty' you were pretty much expected conditioning-wise to be able to go the whole game. We relied on no more than six players."[106]

That philosophy, keeping his best five on the floor as much as possible, became a Driesell staple and one he would continue while rebuilding Davidson in the late 1960s and later at three other schools. "I probably under-substituted my whole career," he has admitted. "I just believed you gotta know who your best five players are and keep 'em together as much and as long as possible. I never agreed with automatically taking a guy out when he got two fouls in the first half or three early in the second. Good players learn how to play with fouls."[107]

6

Pioneering in the South

With the graduation of Dick Snyder in 1966 preceded by the departures of his other, earliest stars, Driesell's Wildcats experienced their one lean year in the mid-1960s, going 15–12 in 1966–1967. Nevertheless, they still made the finals of the Southern Conference Tournament. Several things factored into the drop-off, not the least of which was the unexpected departure of two talented recruits, Bobby Lane from Louisiana and Scott Sinnock from Indiana, both of whom would play only one varsity season before leaving the team due to loss of interest or the chance to pursue other, more surprising dreams. In Sinnock's case, he wanted to become a forest ranger.[108]

It was during this brief lull that Driesell's recruitment of Charles Scott, a New Yorker playing for a black prep school in Laurinburg, North Carolina, began. A straight-A student who applied for early admission to Davidson by placing a $100 deposit, Scott was the first black recruit of an all-white college in the South and his recruitment by "Lefty" Driesell made headlines.[109] "'Lefty' is a great coach and I still think of him as a good friend," Scott has stated.

> I attended his basketball camp at Davidson and he offered me a scholarship when I was still a junior in high school. Up until then, most of the good black players had automatically looked north to the Big Ten and other northern schools. The fact that "Lefty" recruited me opened things up for black players all over the South. I've always told people if there hadn't been a "Lefty" Driesell, there wouldn't have been a Charlie Scott.[110]

That's not to say the relationship between Scott, a 10-year NBA veteran, and Driesell was never somewhat strained. What else could have been expected after Scott's eventual signing with the University of North Carolina at Chapel Hill and its legendary coach Dean Smith after committing to "Lefty" and applying at Davidson? He would go on to earn All-American status in back-to-back years as the first black star in the Tar Heels' rich basketball firmament.[111] When asked about that seminal decision over five decades later, Scott explained it this way: consider his situation at that time, a transcendent star at an all-black prep school with a black coach who, although he didn't push him to go to North Carolina, nevertheless realized the significance of "the state university" finally recruiting an African-American player and "didn't allow him to go any-where else" until he had fully considered UNC. Frank McDuffy was that coach and although there were up to 30 southern schools eventually recruiting Scott out of 108 nationally, it was McDuffy who made sure North Carolina stayed in the final mix along with Davidson, Duke, Wake Forest, and North Caro-lina State, and ultimately made Scott see the influence and social impact he could have by choosing the Tar Heels. "My high school coach was much more aware of those kinds of things than I was," Scott confided. "He was cognizant of what it would mean to be the first black player at UNC—to be the first Black to receive an athletic scholarship there. You have to remember how it was in the South at that time. There was no integration yet, so without just coming out and saying it, he made me sense how important the opportunity was."[112]

At the same time, Scott still doubts he would have been the sought-after, pioneering recruit he was had it not been for "Lefty" Driesell. He said,

"Lefty" was the one who made me feel like it was possible for a black kid to go to a traditionally white school in the South. He even told me about the other players he was recruiting and how he was willing to let me help decide who to go after if I came to Davidson. Don't get me wrong, Coach Smith became my mentor, but that doesn't take away from the influence "Lefty" had on my life. There's no doubt his recruitment of me opened doors for black kids in the South. He will always be a dear friend.[113]

At the time Scott applied for early admission to Davidson (after averaging nearly 27 points per game and leading Laurinburg Institute to a 22–1 record in what was then a Negro prep league entirely separate from the all-white high school competition in North Carolina), a headline in the *Charlotte Observer* read, "Negro Cage Star Applies for Admission to Davidson." And the first two sentences said it all: "Charles Scott, a 6-foot, 5-inch Negro basketball star with All-American potential, has applied for admission to Davidson College. 'Lefty' Driesell confirmed the application and added, 'To say we're pleased would be an understatement.'"[114]

A few weeks later, following his change of heart and switch to the Tar Heels, another story in the *Newport Daily News* was headed, "Scott Explains Why He Picked Carolina" and included a different explanation. It said, "What impressed me about Carolina was that at Chapel Hill you find all types of people. At Davidson there was only a certain, high-class element. In this world you have to learn to live with all kinds, so as far as I personally was concerned, I thought Carolina would provide a better all-around background." That story also gave credit to Carolina Assistant Coach John Lotz for his recruitment of Scott, especially since the deeply religious Scott was "tremendously impressed" by the fact Lotz was married to evangelist Billy Graham's daughter and the fact he was the older brother of Billy Graham Crusade participant Danny Lotz, who previously starred on North Carolina's 1957 national championship team.[115]

A devout Christian and churchgoer himself, Driesell nevertheless agreed that such personal connections probably helped sway Scott as did, perhaps, an unfortunate episode that occurred during one of his visits to Davidson. The way Driesell explained it, he was eating lunch at a local diner when his assistant coach showed up with Scott and they decided to join him. The only problem, unbeknownst to them, the management at this southern eatery still enforced separate sections for its patrons based on the color of their skin and attempted to reseat them in the back part of the restaurant due to Scott's presence at their table. Needless to say, Driesell was immediately angry and they all left. To this day, he bemoans the fact he "should have been smarter" and known of the segregated rules at that particular establishment. "Although he's never said anything about it, I can't help but think that probably hurt us with Charlie at the time," Driesell said. "It certainly didn't help."[116]

But while Driesell's first African-American recruit would cast his lot with another program and eventually come back to haunt him and his Wildcats, his second one would pay major dividends for Davidson. In fact, Mike Maloy, a 6-foot, 7-inch post player from New York City, would prove to be the same kind of catalyst in the second half of the decade that Hetzel had been in the first, propelling the Wildcats back to Top 10 rankings while leading them to three straight Southern Conference Championships and two Elite Eights, only one win away from the NCAA Final Four. Maloy would finish his career as Davidson's all-time leading rebounder (and scorer until passed by current NBA star Stephen Curry) and like Hetzel, a three-time

All-American. His career scoring average of 19.3 points per game included a 24.6 mark as a junior in 1968–1969, when Davidson finished a best ever 27–3. The total record for his three years of varsity play was 73–13 (24–5 as sophomore, 22–5 as senior). When "Lefty" first called to inform him that Scott would not be joining them after all at Davidson, where they had tentatively planned to be roommates, his disappointed but immediate response was, "That's okay coach…we'll just have to beat his butt."[117]

Wayne Huckel, a talented 6-foot, 3-inch wing player and three-year starter in his own right, was one year ahead of Maloy and fellow 1966 recruits Jerry Kroll from Texas and Doug Cook of New Jersey, who would join the New Yorker to form a solid nucleus for three years. Huckel remembered their impact following the down season the year before. "We had not been very strong up front when I was a sophomore. We lacked balance, but we improved a lot and when those new guys were ready to move up to the varsity. We knew we were going to be pretty good," he said. "Maloy was definitely the frontrunner from an athletic standpoint, what you would call a natural, but we were all very compatible on the court and comfortable playing together from the very beginning."[118]

At 6 feet, 5 inches, Kroll played the wing opposite Huckel. Cook, a burly 6-foot, 6-inch forward, manned the double post along with Maloy, and Huckel's classmate, Dave Moser, was another quality ball-handler for Driesell in the mold of Barry Teague, a point guard who wasn't expected to score much but who did a great job of distributing the ball and running the fast break. Along with Malloy, Huckel (11.7), Kroll (13.9), and Cook (14.5) were all double-figure scorers throughout their varsity careers. Rodney Knowles, a 6-foot, 9-inch starter the previous two years, provided valuable support as a senior off the bench and he, too, would finish as a double-figure scorer for his career (16.0).[119]

"We knew the coaches were excited about our potential, but we were so young, we really didn't think about national rankings too much," Huckel remembered.

> We were just focused on playing one game at a time and learning as we went. "Lefty's" objective was always to get the ball down low and none of us, except maybe Kroll, were what I would consider great outside shooters, so we worked hard at running our offense, rebounding, and getting the ball out on the break. It wasn't long before Coach had us confident we could run with anybody.

Also recruited out of New Jersey after considering Dartmouth and Princeton, Huckel was another excellent student who wanted more from his college years than just an Ivy League education, and the chance to combine the good academics of Davidson with the nationally ranked level of play that Driesell had established was too much for him to pass up, even if it meant going further from home than his family preferred.[120] Following graduation, he would go on to Law School after narrowly missing a Rhodes Scholarship, a near miss that Driesell has often referred to in connection to the two Rhodes Scholars he did coach, one at Davidson (Danny Carrell) and one at Maryland (Tom McMillen). Like Huckel, 10 other players on Driesell's nine Davidson teams would go on to become attorneys while seven others entered the medical field either as physicians, dentists, or surgeons.[121]

With former Wildcat star Terry Holland by then serving as "Lefty's" first full-time assistant coach, Davidson finished eighth in the final 1967–1968 Associated Press poll ahead of perennial powers like Louisville (ninth), Duke (10th), and Kansas. One year later (1968–1969) the Wildcats finished third, their highest final ranking ever behind only UCLA and North Carolina.[122] Unfortunately, it was the same North Carolina team led by that same Charlie Scott that would prove their nemesis in back-to-back years, knocking them out of trips to the Final Four both times with 70–66 and 87–85 Elite Eight wins. As cruel fate would have it, Scott almost singlehandedly carried North Carolina to victory in the second and final of those two meetings by connecting on 10 of 14 shots in the second half, including the winning 20-footer with only three seconds left.[123] "Looking back, I've often wondered why the things that stick with you the longest are the things that went bad like those two regional finals against North Carolina," Huckel reminisced. "Too many of us, UNC is still the devil reincarnate and it's always seemed amazing that Charlie Scott, the guy who was supposed to join us at Davidson, is the guy who ultimately knocked us out of going to the Final Four."[124]

Forebodingly, that second loss to Carolina occurred in Cole Field House at College Park, Maryland, home court for the University of Maryland. Following the game, Terrapins Athletic Director Jim Kehoe invited both "Lefty" and Joyce to come to his home, where he offered Driesell his head basketball coaching position in the Atlantic Coast Conference. Having just lost a regional finals, Driesell at first asked for time to consider, but Kehoe's persistence and his intention to turn to local high school legend Morgan Wooten of DeMatha High School if "Lefty" didn't accept, led the ultimate program builder to take the challenge, leaving a Davidson program that would return Maloy, Kroll, and Cook for an ACC program that hadn't had a winning season in years. "I never regretted leaving Davidson," Driesell stated. "My goal was to put Davidson basketball on the map and we had done that. Every player I recruited at

Davidson had been on a Top 10 team at least once during their college careers." The same would be true at Maryland.[125]

Although originally scheduled to follow "Lefty" to Maryland and remain his assistant coach with the Terrapins, Holland was eventually named the head coach at Davidson at an even younger age (27) than Driesell had been nine years earlier. In a little known scenario, however, Holland's succession as Wildcat boss was on hold for about three months while Larry Brown, a former North Carolina star and at the time an American Basketball Association (ABA) veteran, at first took the job before deciding to continue his professional playing career instead (Brown would later become a famous coach for both college and the pros). Holland had no problem being the fallback choice, taking "Lefty's" leftovers and leading them to another NCAA Tournament. Although never reaching the success level of his mentor, Holland would remain the head coach at Davidson for four more winning seasons before advancing to greater things as the head coach at the University of Virginia. "Coach Driesell was a great mentor for me," Holland stated. "He not only gave me a chance to play on great teams, but to help coach great teams as well."[126]

Meanwhile, despite starring through his senior season, Maloy never graduated. Reputed to be the first African-American Sigma Chi Fraternity pledge in the United States, he always seemed to fit in well on the otherwise all-white campus, but after being drafted by the Boston Celtics and playing three years in the ABA instead, he left to play professionally in Europe and never returned. He became an Austrian citizen and even turned what Huckel described as "musical talents to match his athletic ones" into a lead singing career with the Boring Blues Band. He also taught at the American International School of Vienna. Rumor had it that before leaving this country he had fathered a son in New York, but until reports of a mysterious flu-like illness that claimed his life reached Davidson, no one knew for sure. According to Huckel, that's when a reunion of those great Davidson teams in 2011 produced a memorial to their famous but fallen teammate and the emergence of his son, who enjoyed the chance to learn of his long lost father's basketball accomplishments. "Turns out the son didn't hear about his father until later in life, but I think we all really enjoyed filling him in," Huckel said.[127]

For instance, once when the team was slated to play in New York City at Madison Square Garden, it became necessary to leave Maloy behind for class. Any more absences and his eligibility would have been in jeopardy. As a result, Driesell made arrangements for someone to pick him up after class and drive him to the Charlotte airport for a later flight. Meanwhile, in New York, 4 p.m. came and went and still no Mike Maloy, amounting to fears he had missed his flight. He finally arrived five minutes before tipoff, explaining he had missed his original ride, which forced him to get to the airport on his own. Nonetheless, he caught a later flight and played the entire game, finishing "with about 24 points, 12 rebounds, and three blocked shots." Such were the legends shared and passed down about Davidson's "natural."[128]

7

Emulating UCLA, Challenging Tobacco Road

There were no such "naturals" as Mike Maloy when "Lefty" Driesell took over at the University of Maryland. Instead, Driesell inherited a team coming off back-to-back eight-win seasons and largely devoid of ACC level talent. Statistically (and somewhat ironically), the best player returning was none other than a Hetzel, Fred's younger brother Will, a 6-foot, 7-inch forward from nearby Washington, D.C., who had averaged 23 points per game and earned second team All-ACC status the year before Driesell arrived.

Driesell's immediate predecessor as head coach, Frank Fellows, had rather obviously not gotten the job done, producing a 16–34 mark in his only two years at the helm. He had followed the more successful H. A. "Bud" Milliken, who Fellows played for in the early 1950s.

Milliken's last year, 1966–1967, had ended only 11–14, but he had enjoyed more success previously, finishing with winning seasons in 12 of his 17 years as head coach. Nonetheless, only two of his teams ever exceeded 20 wins and achieved national rankings. The 1953–1954 Terrapin quintet was 23–7 and ranked 20th in the final poll, while the 1957–1958 squad, generally regarded as the school's best prior to "Lefty," was 22–7, ACC Tournament champs, and ranked sixth nationally.[129]

In Maryland's online basketball media guide, that team is listed as the school's first "Team of Tradition,"[130] but the Terps' basketball legacy had never attained the upper echelon

Division I reputation of the UCLAs, Kentuckys, Dukes, Indianas, Michigans, and North Carolinas, the teams followers of the sport automatically looked to when preseason expectations and rankings were annually announced. Although located between two major metropolitan areas in Baltimore and Washington, certainly growing hotbeds for the sport, and within easy driving distance of the other East Coast hoop citadels, New York City and Philadelphia, UM remained an underachiever on the college basketball landscape. In fact, the previously mentioned Billy Packer remembered a time as a young Wake Forest assistant coach when he and "Lefty" Driesell (still at Davidson) had sat together during a mutual scouting trip to Cole Field House and remarked on what a shame it was the Terrapins didn't draw better with such a splendid home arena.[131]

Throughout the 1960s, the Terrapins average attendance was only 6,570 per game. By prompting the administration to insert seats closer to the court, creating a much better home court advantage, and other promotional ideas, Driesell's first team would average over 3,000 more per game (9,900) and go on to exceed 12,000 in average attendance for the next eight straight years. In fact, only once (1981–1982) did average home attendance slip below 10,000 the remainder of his 17 Maryland years. He recounted how

> Cole Field House had originally been built to host boxing, so they could add lots of seats around the ring in the center of the floor. For basketball, the students were too far from the court, so I told Kehoe I wanted to add seats closer. He first said we would have to pay too much for the facilities crew to do that before every game, so I told him my assistant coaches and I would do it if he would let us and for the next four or five games we did.

"Lefty" continued, "It took us a couple of extra hours each time and even the cheerleaders started to help. It got our fans right up to courtside. After Kehoe saw how it helped with the crowd and game atmosphere, he said he would get the facilities people to do it. He realized it was worth it."[132]

Another facility improvement that "Lefty" asked for immediately had to do with his office. "I told Kehoe I needed a basketball office that could compete with other ACC coaches' offices. Frank McGuire was recognized as a big-time coach at South Carolina at the time, so I used him and his office as my example," Driesell said. "Somewhere I had seen carpet on office walls and it looked so nice that I told Kehoe that's what I wanted. Kehoe came back with 'where I come from they put carpet on the floor,' but he made every effort to do everything we needed to be competitive in the ACC."[133]

Jay McMillen, who lettered at Maryland in the mid-1960s and understood the program's recent past and unrealized potential, was among those Kehoe introduced to Driesell early on, an introduction that provided immediate (and future) dividends. It was his observation about Maryland's location in a heavily populated, urban area near the Atlantic Seaboard being similar to that of NCAA champion UCLA and the dynasty it was in the midst of creating on the West Coast that prompted Driesell to make his now famous press conference pronouncement about becoming "the UCLA of the East."[134] According to the *Baltimore Sun*, his actual quote that day read, "I think I can build Maryland into the UCLA of the East Coast, maybe even better than UCLA."[135]

An obvious attention-getter, it was the kind of remark most new coaches would never make (or even consider), but it illustrated perfectly the confidence Driesell brought to his new job. Never again would Maryland accept ACC also-ran status.

With "Lefty" in charge, expectations rose immediately and he wouldn't have wanted it any other way.

With the resulting target squarely on his back, he began to build the only way he knew how—by challenging, outworking, and outcoaching his opposition. After taking "little Davidson" to heights no one previously thought possible, it wasn't a stretch to believe he could work similar miracles at Maryland and he certainly believed it himself. For "Lefty" Driesell, the UCLA statement was actually a declaration of war. With far greater resources than he had ever had before, he was going to war with the other basketball powers of the ACC and he wanted everyone to know it.

No one questioned where the league's power resided. In fact, there was a name for it—Tobacco Road—and no one was more familiar with the outreach of its tentacles on the college basketball mindset than Driesell, who had already gone toe-to-toe with the Dukes, Wakes, N.C. States, and North Carolinas of the ACC in terms of interest, coverage, players, and especially reputation during his time and close proximity at Davidson. "We didn't have the name or tradition of the Dukes and Carolinas, but we had been competitive with those teams, so there was absolutely no reason in my mind to think that we couldn't be at Maryland," he emphasized.

> I didn't have to be reminded of what I was up against. When you are at one of those places, a North Carolina, a Duke, an Indiana, or Kentucky, you are always in the running for the best players in the nation. I was never at a place like that, but that didn't mean I couldn't go after them and get a few. At Maryland, my assistants were assigned to different parts of the country and we recruited nationally. My philosophy was to recruit as many as we could and hopefully get enough of the best ones to compete. If we did that, I had enough

confidence in my coaching to believe we could be one of the best teams in the nation every year. That was my goal.[136]

In another pioneering move worthy of recognition, Driesell again broke the color barrier, so to speak, with the hiring of George Raveling as one of his first two Maryland assistants.[137] A native of nearby Washington, D.C., Raveling was the first African-American coach in the ACC and like Holland, one of many Driesell assistants who would go on to outstanding careers as head coaches in the years and decades to follow. At last count, former Driesell assistants had accumulated about 3,000 wins as college head coaches, including nearly 2,500 at the Division I level.[138]

Joining Raveling on that Terrapin staff was Joe Harrington, a Maryland letterman from the mid-1960s and a close friend and former roommate of Jay McMillen. Harrington was hired as a part-time assistant and intramural director at $8,000 per year, a sum at the time for which he thought he had "died and gone to heaven," and would remain with Driesell through his first 10 seasons in College Park, the longest continuous tenure of any of his assistants. Like Raveling, who would go on to serve as head coach at Washington State, the University of Iowa, and the University of Southern California, Harrington would later be head coach at Hofstra and George Mason Universities, Long Beach State, and the University of Colorado following his time with "Lefty."[139]

Recalling those early days with "Lefty," Harrington said,

Coach (Driesell) always believed and still does that hard work is the key. If an assistant was caught up, he would always say "go work on your scrolls," which were our lists of all the best high school players in the country. Kehoe couldn't believe how much we spent on newspaper subscriptions, keeping up with prospects. He changed Maryland basketball that way. He got us believing that we would win a national championship. He and George (Raveling) made a great team. I was hired after he learned about my special relationship with Jay (McMillen) and our first recruit was Howard White. I knew that first Maryland team wasn't very good and I told him it would be a hard one to coach. "No," he said, "for that reason it would be an easy one to coach; talented teams were much harder to coach." I never forgot he said that, but mainly, I never forgot about his work ethic. Monday mornings were really something. He would arrive early with a legal pad full of notes about what he wanted each assistant to do that week and we were all involved in recruiting, academics, practice, summer camps, weight training, and special projects, of which there were many. At the same time, Coach would never ask you to do something he wasn't willing to do himself. It was his honesty that was foremost. Coach did things within the rules. He had a presence about him that stood out in a crowd, still does, even in his 80s.[140]

One area of the country Driesell and his new staff recognized as being particularly critical to improved recruiting was their own backyard. Like most urban areas, the Beltway was annually home to lots of talented high school basketball players and "Lefty" aimed to keep his share at home. His first Terrapin signing class included one such local star, Jim O'Brien, a talented 6-foot, 8-inch forward from Falls Church, Virginia, but Driesell wanted more and to land O'Brien and three other area standouts, including current NFL TV host James Brown (who ultimately played at Harvard), he concocted a revolutionary recruiting strategy, one that drew national attention. First, however, he had to sell the idea to his athletic director.

"We were doing some crazy stuff when it came to recruiting and came up with the idea of running an ad in the *Washington Post* with pictures of those four guys under the headline, 'Maryland Basketball Wants You' with their names and stats," he recalled fondly.

> I told Kehoe and he quickly said you can't do that, but we had already gone through the NCAA Rule Book and consulted two lawyers and neither we nor they could find anything in there that definitely stated such a thing would be a violation. You've got to remember, that was 1970 and the NCAA Rule Book wasn't nearly as detailed and specific as it is now, and even though something like that had never been done, it wasn't spelled out as being illegal. Well, we finally convinced Kehoe and he said we could do it, and we did. Immediately after the ad came out, we got national publicity from coast to coast. They even ran the ad in other newspapers, including the *Los Angeles Times*, to show what we trying to get away with and pretty soon people were saying "what the crap does 'Lefty' think he's doing?" It also wasn't long before the NCAA got in touch with Kehoe and said we couldn't do that, but our lawyers went to Kansas City and the NCAA later had to admit there was no specific rule at the time that prohibited it. Eventually, it just kind of died away, but in the meantime we got tremendous publicity out of the idea. O'Brien was the only one of those players we signed, but for a first-year program, the publicity was great.[141]

Even in his first, breakeven year at Maryland (13–13), 1969–1970, the Terrapins had some good wins, including victories over Duke, Virginia, and West Virginia. It was in his second season, however, that the Terps provided the first truly signature win of the "Lefty" Driesell era despite their second lowest scoring total ever, a 31–30 victory over McGuire's nationally recognized South Carolina Gamecocks. What set the stage for that January 1971 upset was a 26-point loss to those same talent-laden Gamecocks in mid-December at Columbia, South Carolina.[142]

Still in the ACC in those days, South Carolina had some big-name players, including three-time All-American John Roche, and with three or four minutes left in that first meeting, they appeared headed to a coliseum scoring record when a fight broke out. According to Driesell, other fights broke out almost immediately and even he, the visiting coach, took a punch while trying to break up the melee that ensued. "It was nearly a riot and police had to come and escort our team off the floor," he said. "The game was called with about three or four minutes left and South Carolina leading 96–70. Afterwards, I made the comment I couldn't wait for their return visit to Cole Field House the following month."[143]

In fact, McGuire was hesitant to bring his team north for the rematch and said so, but he was assured by the Maryland administration that steps would be taken to maintain order when the Gamecocks arrived at Cole on 9 January. As a result, Driesell has long remembered the return visit as follows:

Every coach in America knew that whenever Frank (McGuire) was ahead or tied, he would sit back in a 2–3 zone defense, so I told my point guard, Howard White, to just hold the ball if they did that against us. They were a lot bigger and more talented than we were and that was before the shot clock, so I was happy to just let the clock run. That's what we did the whole first half and just before the buzzer, Howard hit a shot to put us up 4–3 at halftime. In the second half, they came out in a man-to-man, but we were still able to stay out of a running game and keep it close (there were seven ties in second half) and when we successfully executed a play we had worked on if we ever needed to miss a free throw on purpose, where we would bring a guy down the baseline for a tip-in (O'Brien's tip of White's miss), we somehow got the game into overtime. In overtime, they built a five point lead (30–25), but with 24 seconds left, O'Brien scored to cut the lead to three (30–27) and I got a quick timeout so I could put

Dick Stobaugh, our tallest player at 6 feet, 8 inches, on the guy taking the ball out against our press, which was Roche. Amazingly, for a player as good as he was, Roche tried to make a difficult pass and Howard picked it off and got it back to Dick right under the basket for an easy layup that cut their lead to one (30–29). Again, I got a time out to set up the press and this time Bob Bodell cut in front of one of their guys, intercepted another inbounds pass, and got it to Howard, who found O'Brien just off the left baseline. There was a famous picture taken from behind Jim after he let the shot go, which clearly shows the ball in the air and all our fans under the basket watching, hoping it goes in (O'Brien finished six for six from the field). When it did, they were so happy, they literally tore that goal down (ala football goal posts) and we had to buy a completely new stanchion and have it installed before out next game. That was the start of big things at Maryland.[144]

So big in fact, that with attendance, interest, and enthusiasm building, Driesell began to extend both arms and hold up two fingers on both hands (as in Winston Churchill's famous V for victory sign) whenever he appeared courtside after pregame warm-ups. Taking that as their cue, the Terrapin pep band also started playing "Hail to the Chief." It was unprecedented showmanship at College Park and the fans loved it. In fact, it became such an anticipated part of Maryland's pregame, home court ritual that the Terps' Washington neighbors at 1600 Pennsylvania Avenue eventually requested the band to cease and desist as a matter of respect, since that tune is supposedly reserved for the President. Lucky for Richard Nixon, "Lefty" had his own job to do and wasn't bothered by losing his theme song.[145]

One of those new fans suddenly hooked on Maryland basketball was, actually, someone who covered the Nixon White House on a regular basis, Washington columnist Robert

Novak, who would write about attending an upset of Duke in his 2007 book *The Prince of Darkness*. In it he documented, "When I entered the arena that night I was not even sure which team I wanted to win. But then and there I became a Maryland fan. The Driesell Era had begun and I was hooked." The next year, Novak had season tickets and remained a diehard fan (and friend) throughout "Lefty's" Terrapin tenure.[146]

As fate would have it, Maryland's first game in the 1970–1971 ACC Tournament would be with that same South Carolina juggernaut the Terps had embarrassed in College Park and this time talent would prevail, 71–63, but not before "Lefty" sought to again outfox McGuire by having his players switch jerseys. He explained,

> I knew they had been studying film of us, so I had everybody change numbers and it messed them up for awhile. Problem was who it really messed up was all the radio and TV people covering the game. Now there's a rule that even in practice you can't change player jerseys. It was just another idea I had to try and gain a slight advantage against a team we otherwise didn't have much chance of beating, but it drove the media crazy. Needless to say, they weren't real happy with me that night.[147]

On the other hand, Maryland fans were unusually happy about a mere one-game improvement to 14–13 his second year because waiting in the wings was one of the best freshmen teams in the country, an undefeated group that would propel the Terrapins to five straight 20-plus win seasons and feature players who would become household names among college basketball fans during the mid-1970s. They would be led by the nation's No. 1 recruit, a studious 6-foot, 11-inch "phenom" from Mansfield, Pennsylvania, Tom McMillen; and his equally cerebral sidekick from the streets of New York, Len Elmore.

Together they would give "Lefty" Driesell the equal of any frontcourt in America.[148]

8

Madness at Midnight, Frustration in March

As recently as October 2012, a contributing writer for *Forbes* magazine, Alicia Jessop, recalled the start of Midnight Madness, the now traditional kickoff for college basketball practices all across the United States. For over 30 years, it always began at the stroke of midnight on 15 October, the first day full team practices were permitted by the NCAA. Now a televised event, it was designed to get students excited and involved with their college teams as quickly as possible, and as Jessop documented (like several others before her), it was the brainchild of Charles "Lefty" Driesell.

Setting the stage, she wrote:

> Forty-one years ago on an autumn night in College Park, Maryland, the landscape of college basketball changed forever. On 15 October 1971, legendary college basketball coach "Lefty" Driesell and his staff drove their cars around midnight to Byrd Stadium at the University of Maryland campus. The sky was as dark as the night was late, but the tireless competitor Driesell had a plan to maximize the amount of time that the NCAA bylaws allowed his team to practice so it could achieve the success he believed to be possible.[149]

Driesell had good reason to want as early a start as possible for the 1971–1972 season. After two years of being just one game over .500 in his new job at the University of Maryland, he was about to unleash a new brand of Terrapins sparked by the addition to varsity status of what had been one of the best freshmen teams in the nation the year before, an advent the entire UM community had been anxiously awaiting for more than a year. Headlining the new additions would be Tom McMillen and Len Elmore, 6-foot, 11-inch and 6-foot, 9-inch giants, respectively, one white and one black and both exemplary students who would represent the program in the best way possible for years to come. Who could have blamed Driesell for wanting to get off to the earliest start possible on the new season now that he had "the horses" to actually contend with Tobacco Road for ACC and even national honors?[150]

That October night in 1971, Driesell actually began his first practice the way he always had, by requiring his players to run one mile in less than six minutes. The only difference: he did it on the very first minute of the first day practice could legally begin in order to begin his regular practice the following afternoon without the need for his standard conditioning test, thereby getting his new team (and new stars) involved in basketball drills and teamwork sooner than would otherwise have been possible—a jump on the competition, so to speak.

So with his and his assistant coaches' car lights providing enough light at the corners of the track for the players to stay on course as they executed their required mile run, the first opening midnight practice in NCAA basketball history took place. Unbeknownst to Driesell and his coaches, however, a sizeable contingent of Maryland students had learned of the midnight run and like passionate college students everywhere with nothing better to do on a weekday night, especially in anticipation of their new, nationally ranked Terps, an estimated 2,000 were on hand to see for themselves.[151] There's even a famous photo of Driesell, Raveling, and longtime Maryland Sports Information Director Jack Zane at the dimly lit finish line with stop watches in hand as each player completed their individually timed runs.[152]

Needless to say, it was an eye-opening experience for a coach with the promotional savvy of Driesell and later, when one of his players stated the obvious—if that many students would come out for nothing more than a conditioning run, why not stage a full team scrimmage after the run and see how many more that would draw?—the head coach didn't have to think twice about how practice would open in 1972–1973, which it did with about 8,000 in the field house stands. Such was the genesis of Midnight Madness, a concept top teams have since adopted to the point of light shows, fog machines, and performances by major recording artists. According to Jessop's article, basketball rich University of Kansas alone was expected to draw 16,300 for Midnight Madness in 2012 and such crowds have become equally typical at places like Kentucky, Syracuse, and North Carolina. "I should have trademarked the idea," Driesell has joked on many occasions since.[153]

Actually, imaginative promotions like Midnight Madness became commonplace at Maryland under the inspired leadership of Russ Potts, one of the nation's first great college promoters and a future Virginia state senator, but Driesell knew that ultimately only talented players would put the Terrapins on top and keep them there. That's what made the signings of Tom McMillen and Len Elmore so important. Just as losing Charlie Scott to Dean Smith and North Carolina proved a tremendous blow to Driesell's hopes at Davidson, so too "Lefty" absconding with the nation's No. 1 recruit just a few years later, a recruit who had been a regular at Smith's North Carolina basketball camps for years, shook up the hoops universe and established Maryland as a new force to be reckoned with (just as Hetzel's presence had done 10 years earlier at Davidson).

"The reason I got Tom was his brother (Jay) and his father," Driesell has admitted on many occasions. "Not only had Jay played at Maryland and was one of our best supporters, but his father, who was ill, wanted him to stay close to home so he wouldn't have to travel far to see him play."[154]

Home for the McMillens was near the New York state border—not particularly close to College Park, but a whole lot closer than Chapel Hill, North Carolina. "Everybody was on McMillen," Driesell confirmed.

> He was valedictorian of his senior class and a straight-A student. Along with us and North Carolina, he was considering Virginia and Pennsylvania of the Ivy League. In fact the first time I met Tom, he told me the University of Pennsylvania had three million books in its library and UNC had two million, while Maryland only had a million. I told him if he read all of those, I would make sure we got some more. Kehoe, who had been at Maryland for 25 years, was with me that night and as we left the McMillen home, he commented, "There's no way that kid is coming to Maryland."[155]

That same year, Dean Smith was also recruiting 7-foot, 4-inch Tom Burleson, who would go on to a great career at North Carolina State. Smith envisioned a very tall and talented double post, featuring McMillen and Burleson, and he was hoping the former would actually assist in signing the latter. "When Tom's father got wind of that, I don't think he liked it and told Dean so, even though Tom had verbally committed to UNC with a big press conference just over the state line in Elmira, New York," Driesell recalled.

So Dean flies up there in a private plane with a letter of intent, but his parents both insisted they weren't going to sign for him to go to North Carolina and as everyone knows, it's no good without a parent's signature. His father, bless his soul, even put notes under Tom's bedroom door about why he didn't want him at UNC, which drove Tom crazy. At one time, I even told his father, who was a dentist, "Doc, Dean is really not that bad a guy," but he was adamant about not wanting Tom to go that far from home.

Driesell added,

At the same time, I think Tom's mother wanted him to go to the University of Virginia because she liked the coach there at the time, Bill Gibson. In fact, the day he decided he was coming to Maryland, Gibson was at his house. At some point, I just stayed in the background and left our recruitment to his brother. That's when Jay told him, "If you don't go to Maryland, I will never speak to you again." It's still hard to believe Dean didn't get either Tom or Burleson. North Carolina was not used to getting shut out like that.[156]

In his 1992 book, *Out of Bounds*, McMillen discussed that critical (and unfortunately very confrontational) period in his life and also gave credit to Maryland's location as a factor in his ultimate decision. "Another ingredient in my decision was the proximity of Maryland to Washington, D.C.," he stated.

In my senior year of high school, President Nixon had appointed me as the youngest member ever on the President's Council on Physical Fitness and Sports, and I had been bitten by the political bug. That and "Lefty" shrewdly reminded me that if I played for the Terps, the President of the United States would be reading of my exploits in the *Washington Post* every day.[157]

Such a saga exemplified the inherent pressure of being regarded as a transformational recruit and McMillen, who was ranked that year ahead of even eventual college legend Bill Walton (UCLA), was certainly considered that and more. "So the last day to register for fall classes, Jay calls me about noon and says 'Coach, my car is packed with Tom's stuff and he's coming to Maryland, but he doesn't want a big to-do or anything. He just wants to show up, register, and get in his room without the press and everybody else being involved,'" Driesell remembered. "So I hang up the phone and I'm going crazy I'm so excited. I tell the assistants 'we got him, we got him,' but in the next breath I'm telling them to keep this as low key as possible."

It was about a three-hour drive from the McMillen home to College Park and Driesell remembered the last-minute scramble to find his No. 1 recruit a dorm room, preferably a private one. Such a room was finally located on the fourth floor of the dorm occupied by the Maryland football team. "I don't think Dean was ever bitter and every time we played North Carolina the next several years, he would give Tom a hug. They've had a good relationship ever since just like I've had with Charlie Scott," Driesell stated. But it wasn't that way for the North Carolina fans. The first year the Terrapins went to Chapel Hill with McMillen on the team, "Lefty" recalled people holding signs that read, "Tom, call your mother," mocking him for signing with Maryland after committing to the Tar Heels.[158]

At the same time, Elmore, a product of New York City's Power Memorial, the same high school that had produced UCLA's legendary Lew Alcindor (later Kareem Abdul-Jabbar) just a few years before, was a top 20 recruit on an unbeaten team with a number of college prospects. "We were actually recruiting him and a teammate," Driesell recalled.

Elmore was a great shot blocker and like Tom, a very good student who at one time expressed a desire to go to an Ivy League school like Princeton. I also had a pretty good reputation in the New York area because of the Davidson players I had recruited up there and there was a guy in real estate, Sam LaFrak, a Maryland graduate who owned most of the city's rental properties and he took Lenny, Tom, and I to the Lotus Club, a big-time place in downtown New York, and sold him on UM. Lenny wanted to be an attorney and he even sold him on the idea that he could help him become a judge in New York someday. Needless to say, "Lefty," LeFrak, and the Lotus Club did a sales job that Elmore couldn't refuse and the double coup, along with McMillen, became the stuff of legend in recruiting circles.[159]

Together they combined to lead the Terrapins to 27–5, 22–6, and 23–5 records from 1971–1972 through 1973–1974, unprecedented success up to that time in school annals and three straight Top 15 finishes (14th in 1972, 8th in 1973, 4th in 1974). Unfortunately, they would also suffer through three straight frustrating defeats in the ACC Tournament Finals, including what most hoops historians consider the greatest college game ever played in 1974. In two of those losses, the Terps narrowly missed NCAA Tournament bids due to the fact (as previously established) that before 1974 only conference champions advanced to an NCAA field of between 22 and 25 teams. In fact, most credit that iconic 1974 ACC Championship with bringing about the first expansion of the NCAA Tournament to 32 teams, allowing for more than one team from what was considered deserving, "power conferences," of which the ACC was certainly one (in 1973 Maryland did advance to the NCAA despite its ACC tourney finals loss, as ACC champ North Carolina State was serving a probation and thus ineligible to participate).[160]

Career highlights for the duo included the championship of the National Invitational Tournament their first varsity season at a time when the NIT at New York's Madison Square Garden still meant more than it does today due to the NCAA Tournament's much smaller field and more restrictive selection process. In other words, back then many of the nation's best teams advanced to the NIT after individual losses or upsets in conference play. In addition, Driesell's McMillen-Elmore led 1973 team, the ACC runner-up, would lose in the East Regional Finals to No. 4 Providence (103–89) after knocking off No. 14 Syracuse (91–75).[161]

Actually, by the time McMillen's college career started, he had already received more attention than any other Maryland basketball player ever despite having not played a single game. He had already been on the covers of national magazines, including *Sports Illustrated*, and his high school uniform had already been retired to the Naismith Memorial Basketball Hall of Fame after he averaged 47.7 points and 22.2 rebounds per game as a prep senior. He would go on to average 20.8 points per game as a sophomore, 21.2 as a junior, and 19.4 as a senior,[162] the year his father died at Christmas time and also the year he applied for and received his Rhodes Scholarship. At the same time he averaged nearly 10 rebounds per game for his career.[163] In Dave Ungrady's book, *Legends of Maryland Basketball*, McMillen is quoted as saying, "The best thing about attending Maryland was the totality of the experience. It wasn't just playing basketball, it was most meaningful to me to win the Rhodes Scholarship and although we never lived up to the UCLA of the East moniker, we did set the precedent and opened it up so that Maryland could win the championship years later (NCAA champs in 2002)." He would go on to play for the U.S. Olympic team, in the NBA for 11 years with four different teams (Buffalo Braves, New York Knicks, Atlanta Hawks, Washington Bullets), and represent Maryland's fourth district in Congress for six years.[164]

Meanwhile, after injuries slowed Elmore (and the team) at the start of his sophomore year, he first established himself in the championship of Maryland's holiday tournament against his highly ranked hometown rivals from St. Johns University, a game in which he would grab almost 20 rebounds, block 10 shots, and be named the tournament MVP. He would also score 23 points and grab 14 rebounds in the NIT Semifinals against Jacksonville, and block 11 shots in the NIT Championship win over Niagara. For his three-year career, he would average 11.8 points and 12.2 rebounds, which is still the school record. He would also play 10 years in the ABA and NBA with the Indiana Pacers, Kansas City Kings, Milwaukee Bucks, New Jersey Nets, and New York Knicks; earn a Law Degree from Harvard University; and become one of network television's most respected college basketball analysts. In Ungrady's book, Elmore stated, "We knew there was no conference as tough as the ACC and we had beaten some of the best teams in the country in conference play. That tournament (NIT) in March of our sophomore year opened our eyes to our potential as a team and for me as an individual (player)."[165]

While Elmore and McMillen were the constants in Driesell's starting lineup throughout that three-year run—"the two frontcourt stars boosting 'Lefty's' legions from mediocrity to might," according to eloquent columnist Dick Heller in the 8 March 2004 *Washington Star*—they also featured trusted veterans in O'Brien, Bodell, and guard Maurice Howard, and had added the likes of 6-foot, 6-inch Darrell Brown and 6-foot, 9-inch Owen Brown, and eventually the best Maryland guard ever in 6-foot, 4-inch John Lucas. That same 2004 Heller column, written almost 30 years to the day after he covered the last of those title tilts, reminded Beltway readers of just how memorable that game and team really was.

In what really was "a grim and gallant struggle," Heller replayed one more time how that triple overtime game for the ages, which ended 103–100 in North Carolina State's favor, not only pointed N.C. State toward its first national championship, but also how it kept Maryland out of March Madness that year altogether. "Odd as it seems now," Heller stated, "only the tournament champion represented the conference in what was a 25-team NCAA field. So the proud Terrapins turned down a bid to go to the NIT, which they had won two years earlier, and accepted their role as one of the best teams ever to miss the NCAAs." What could now be added to that statement as a postscript is the fact they were also one of the best teams never to win an NCAA title. "It's amazing how many people saw (that) game, either then or on ESPN Classic," Heller's story quoted Elmore. And despite the fact it was such a devastating loss, he added, "I don't mind at all—I'm (still) proud to have been a part of it."[166]

In addition, the 2002 book entitled *Maryland Basketball* addressed what Paul McMullen headlined "The Greatest Game" and the frustration those Terps felt at becoming the only team to lose three straight ACC Tournament championship games. In it, he referenced how McMillen "howled" about the inequities of Tobacco Road and always having to play the tournament in Greensboro, North Carolina. That frustration would only mount when N.C. State dethroned UCLA in the NCAA Finals a few weeks later, providing the ACC with its only national champion between 1958 and 1981. Later, McMillen's book included a gracious quote from N.C. State Coach Norm Sloan, who said, "His (Driesell's) team shot near

60 percent, scored 100 points, had few turnovers, and still lost. Maryland didn't go to the NCAA Tournament, but they were one of the best teams of the decade, one of the best ever."[167]

Perhaps Driesell voiced the feelings of every ACC coach at the time when he stated,

> You talk about pressure, that was pressure. I think it was a factor in UCLA winning all those NCAA titles (10 in 12 years) because they didn't have to play a (conference) tournament. If you were lucky enough to win three games in the ACC Tournament in those days, you were wrung out. That's when the ACC Tournament really had some meaning. Now it's just a fundraiser. It's still exciting, but not like it used to be.[168]

9

From Inside Out with No Moses to Lead Them

The graduations of McMillen and Elmore in 1974 signaled a time for rebuilding, especially for a coach who had always relied on an inside-oriented, double post offense. That fact alone made for a challenging offseason, but didn't keep Driesell from achieving hero status when he earned the NCAA's first Award of Valor by clearing residents from a burning townhouse near his family's vacation home at Bethany Beach, Delaware. "I didn't think it was a big deal at the time; something anybody would have done, but it got a lot of local newspaper coverage. I was surprised when the award came in the mail," he remembered.[169] Such modesty, however, came with renewed focus founded on the return of Lucas, who figured to be one of the best players in the entire country even without his two, towering ex-teammates.

Among the first freshmen to start and star after NCAA freshmen became eligible for football and basketball in 1972, Lucas was a native of Durham, North Carolina, first recommended to Driesell by Paul Williamson, a friend and teacher at East Durham Junior High School. Driesell remembered it this way: "Paul called me and said 'Lefty, you've got to come see this kid,' so I sent George (Raveling) to see one of his games and he came back unimpressed. When I shared that with Paul, he immediately said, 'I don't care what George thinks, he's a heck of a player and a great kid from a great family and if you don't recruit him, I will never speak to you again.'" As a result, Driesell has always been indebted to

Williamson for his insistence and scouting insight, and added, "The first time I saw Lucas play, he got about 30 points in an all-star game. From that point on, there was no doubt in my mind what kind of player he could be."[170]

Lucas would eventually choose Maryland from among hundreds of scholarship offers, including UCLA, and later state, "'Lefty' was the deciding factor for me."[171] As gifted in tennis as he was in basketball (All-American in both), he became a left handed extension of his famous left handed coach, masterfully guiding the offense for four straight years while averaging 14.2 points as a freshman, 20.1 as a sophomore, 19.5 as a junior, and 19.9 as a senior. He would go on to play 14 years in the NBA for six different teams after being the league's first draft pick of the Houston Rockets (1976), a team he would spend three separate tours of duty with and reach the NBA Finals with in 1986.[172] Unfortunately, his final years as a professional player were clouded by drug use and rehabilitation, but he was able to overcome that stigma and become a symbol of recovery by mentoring other athletes struggling with drugs, as well as serving stints as an NBA head coach with the San Antonio Spurs, Philadelphia 76ers, and Cleveland Cavaliers.[173] Proud of his former teammate's recovery, McMillen stated in *Out of Bounds*, "With tremendous strength and courage, John fought back to kick the drug habit and resume his basketball career."[174]

During his final three years at Maryland, Lucas always played on basketball teams ranked no lower than 10th in the nation and as high as No. 2. Twice during his career Maryland would reach the Elite Eight. At the same time, he would win ACC singles titles in tennis twice as well as also being part of a conference doubles championship.[175]

Along with Lucas in what became "Lefty's" restructured, three-guard offense were Howard and Brad Davis, slender 6-foot, 2-inch and 6-foot, 3-inch stars, respectively. Like Lucas, both were quick, excellent ball-handlers, and the Terps' fast-breaking, quick-strike style became a dominant, fun-to-watch college basketball attraction. In fact, the 1975–1976 Maryland team became one of the highest scoring in NCAA history, going over 100 points in seven different games and over 90 in six others. Between 1973–1974, when both Howard and Lucas joined the varsity, and 1976, the last year all three would play together, the Terps would score 100 or more points 21 times.[176]

Howard, a Philadelphia product, would play only one season in the NBA while Davis, after stints with Los Angeles (Lakers), Indiana, and Utah (four years total), would star for the Dallas Mavericks at point guard (his Mavs' jersey is retired) for 11 seasons. His extraordinary backcourt success came despite the fact he played center in high school at little Monaca, Pennsylvania. "One of my assistants in the 1970s, Dave Pritchett, saw him (Davis) play and assured me he was a great passer and ball handler, and could make a great guard," Driesell recounted. "After we had been recruiting him, Bobby Knight saw him play in the Dapper Dan Classic and started recruiting him hard for Indiana, but because we had been in on him early, thanks to Pritchett, we were able to hang on and sign him."[177] As a guard, Davis would connect on a remarkable 54 percent of his field goal attempts at Maryland along with 80 percent at the foul line, while contributing 5.1 assists and 12.2 points per game during his three-year career, which ended with him turning pro after his junior season.[178]

"When Brad came, it allowed me to free up to score more," Lucas once explained.[179] In fact, Davis had to assume an immediate leadership role when Lucas suffered a broken collarbone in their first regular season game together, dramatically increasing his initial playing time as a freshman. Despite the temporary loss of their three-time All-American, the 14–1 Terps lost only once during his absence (to No. 3 UCLA) and by the time Lucas was back, Driesell was truly ready to unleash his three-guard onslaught against defending national champion North Carolina State. What resulted was a decisive, mid-January victory at College Park, a 103–85 win that had other ACC coaches rushing back to their drawing boards, reassessing how to defend "Lefty's" new look.[180]

By that time an assistant for Driesell, Howard White remembered the three guard approach as a "big advantage." He said,

> We were hard to defend. It gave us quickness and presented real matchup problems for most of the teams we played, and Brad had always had to guard bigger people, so it wasn't that much of a stretch for him to pick up the other team's smallest forward. In those days, "Lefty" had a fiery personality and if he thought something would work, he worked hard to make sure everyone on the team felt the same way. He made sure we all believed in what we were doing.[181]

Later that same year, the Terps would again beat the defending champs, snapping a 37-game N.C. State home court winning streak (98–97) in Raleigh with that same personnel grouping, a group some have since termed "The Wild Bunch."[182] They would go on to what was then an NCAA record .547 shooting percentage from the field, breaking the old mark of .544 that just happened to have been previously set by one of Driesell's Davidson teams in 1964.[183] Along with the trio of guards, that new-look lineup included Steve Sheppard, a powerful 6-foot, 6-inch forward who would play on the 1976 Gold Medal U.S. Olympic team, and either Tom Roy or Owen

Brown, both 6 feet, 9 inches. Despite the guard oriented lineup, Sheppard, another New York City native, would average an impressive 16.0 points and 7.7 rebounds for his three-year career.[184] He would also return after two NBA seasons (Chicago Bulls) to finish his degree despite coming to Maryland as a non-predictor. "Just getting to class was a real effort with Steve," Driesell recalled. "He really didn't know how to study, but by his last year he was Academic All-ACC."

But while Sheppard, Roy, and Brown provided some inside balance, it's always been a shame the new look didn't include a teammate from Davis's previously mentioned Dapper Dan Classic, another consensus No. 1 recruit and a transcendent talent that Driesell had been eyeing for some time. Already a prep legend in Driesell's native Virginia because of his dominance at Petersburg High School, Moses Malone was indeed a man among boys at 6 feet, 10 inches, and nearly 230 pounds when "Lefty" first laid eyes on him. "He was a great player who scored 50 points in the first game I ever saw him play," Driesell recalled. "He may have been the greatest rebounder ever. He rarely got a pass. Most of his points came off the offensive boards. After seeing him play, I told my assistants that if we could get this guy, we would win the national championship."

Among those who doubted "Lefty's" descriptions of such a *Promised Land* was Lucas, who couldn't believe that kind of immediate, game-changing recruit existed. "When I first told Lucas about Moses, he couldn't believe there was one guy that good, so I told him he should go down to Petersburg and work out with Moses," Driesell recalled.

> When he did, he rushed back and said "coach you were right, we've got to get that guy." In fact, in those days all the players on scholarship at Maryland got $15 per month

laundry money and Lucas got them together and they all promised their laundry money to Moses if he would sign with us. Nowadays that doesn't sound like much, but for a bunch of college kids in the 1970s that would have been a real sacrifice. It just showed how much they would have loved to have Moses on our team.

Such a frontcourt force might have indeed led the already backcourt blessed Terrapins to the *Promised Land,* but since he was regarded as the best college basketball prospect since Alcindor (aka Abdul-Jabbar), Driesell knew competition for his services would be intense, and he was prepared to act accordingly. "He was such a poor kid," Driesell remembered.

> I'll never forget, he even had a hole in his bedroom wall. His high school coach was a guy named Pro Hayes and after months of recruiting him and sweating through every detail, Hayes calls me and says "Coach Driesell, Moses is ready to sign with you if you come to Petersburg tonight." So we (including assistant coaches) hurried down to Petersburg and checked in at the Holiday Inn. Because Moses was so shy, I told Howard (White) to ride with him and Hayes on the way from the high school to his house and to keep the conversation going so Moses wouldn't change his mind. Pritchett and I followed along behind. We were so afraid that somebody else would still try to get in there and sign him before we could and when we got to his house, where just he and his mother lived, he up and said nobody should go inside yet and for us to come back in the morning and he would sign then.

At this point in his story, Driesell became more animated:

> So Moses goes inside and Pritchett starts moaning, "Oh no, something is wrong." That's when he comes up with the idea of staying in the car all night right there in front of the house to make sure some other coach doesn't show up to try and sign him. Well trying to stay calm, I said no, we should

respect Moses' wishes, but Pritchett insisted so I climbed in the back seat and we stayed there all night. That's how we knew when Chuck Noe, the coach at VCU (Virginia Commonwealth University) and one of his boosters showed up about 6:30 in the morning. Moses' mother let them in. In fact, when we finally went inside, they were all sitting in the living room downstairs. Noe saw us come in and said to the booster, "let's go." But the other guy said, "no way, I'm staying right here until I know he's signed." So with all this going on, Hayes eventually comes in and says "come on Coach Driesell, let's go upstairs to Moses' bedroom and get this done." When we got up there, Moses was still stretched out on his bed and he and his mother signed the letter of intent right there.[185]

Obviously big news throughout the Beltway, Driesell had never felt the need for an unlisted telephone number until word of Malone's decision got out. In fact, the hype machine continued right up until the day before Moses Malone was scheduled to register at College Park. That's when "Lefty" got a phone call he has always regretted, a call from Moses informing him that a representative of the relatively new ABA was at his home and had $10,000 in cash spread on his coffee table, ready to leave it there if he and his mother would agree to a professional contract with the Utah Stars. "Tell him to get out of your house right now and if he's still there in 10 minutes call me back," Driesell can remember exclaiming into the telephone.

Unlike the much more established NBA at the time, the ABA had never sworn off teenage prodigies like Malone, who obviously had the ability to go straight from high school to professional basketball. The new league was just trying to survive and if beating the NBA to future stars like a Moses Malone was one way to do it (even if that meant taking some right out of high school) then so be it. Thinking fast, Driesell reminded Malone that he was worth a lot more than $10,000, maybe even as much as $250,000, and if he was worth that much now, just think how much he would be worth after playing a year or two in college. "I told him that guy was trying to screw him and that we would turn it over to a lawyer, but not to sign anything until we got there," Driesell added. "You have to understand, $10,000 was probably more money than Moses and his mother had ever had all together, much less in one lump sum. I think she was making about $75 a week working in a nursing home, so it wasn't easy for either of them to tell that guy from the ABA they needed some time to think about everything."

A meeting was arranged with Donald Dell, a prominent Washington, D.C., attorney and the eventual founder of ProServ, at the Marriott Hotel near then National Airport. Driesell knew a player of Malone's talents should probably be thinking in terms of million-dollar guaranteed contracts even then and with the NBA's looming move to also signing high school "phenoms" on the horizon, a bidding war could be just around the corner, especially if Malone produced in his first year at Maryland like "Lefty" knew he could. In fact, for a player of Malone's limited economic background and lack of academic motivation, one year of collegiate competition was probably all Driesell could realistically hope for and it quickly became apparent to all involved that his best interests would be served by going pro—immediately.[186]

Shifting gears by putting aside his own dreams on behalf of his young recruit, Driesell worked with Dell to help make that happen in the most equitable and beneficial way possible, something that has never been lost on Malone, who remains one of "Lefty's" best friends and biggest supporters to the present day.[187] At the same time, what might have been has never been lost on Driesell either, as Malone would go on to a star-studded 21-year professional career. Three times after switching leagues he would be named NBA Most Valuable Player and his selection among the NBA's 50 Greatest Players in 1996 was never in doubt.[188] When the ink was officially dry on his first contract, Malone, somewhat remorseful that he would never play for "Lefty," told him a story about how his mother had made him read the Bible every day while growing up and how when he finally got his own copy of the "good book," he had written his goals on the center leaf, including his plan to be the best high school player in America by his junior year and his desire to be the first high school player to go pro. With all that in mind, he informed his would-be coach and mentor that he was indeed afraid "the Lord would punish" him if he didn't turn pro now that the opportunity was actually presented.[189] He would average 18 points and 14 rebounds as a 19-year-old professional rookie.[190]

"If it had all been just one day later, he probably would have been registered, Utah would have been out of luck, and every college credit he attained at Maryland would have been worth a sizeable addition to his first pro contract," Driesell still maintained. "It's my biggest disappointment in recruiting. I've always felt that if we had gotten Moses we could have beaten any of those teams that won national championships in the mid-1970s."[191] As for how he feels about "Lefty," Malone, a 2001 inductee to the Naismith Basketball Hall of Fame, said, "Coach Driesell is a great man. He introduced me to Donald Dell when I needed help. He was like a father figure for me. He was in my corner from the start and made me feel like he would do anything to help me. I have nothing but respect for him." And when asked how Maryland might have done if he had played for the Terrapins, Malone seemed to echo Driesell's original assessment when, without the slightest hesitation, he said, "We would have won two or three NCAA champion-ships...for sure."[192]

Reloading with Buck and Albert

The Lucas-led teams of 1973–1974 through 1975–1976 would go 23–5, 24–5, and 22–6. Only in 1976–1977 after Lucas was gone did the Terrapins fall below the 20-victory mark, finishing 19–11 in Davis's final season, 1976–1977. Driesell needed some time to reload and 1977–1978 would end even worse at 15–13.[193]

Actually, 1977–1978 was also the freshman year for another of Driesell's big recruiting catches, Albert King, the 6-foot, 6-inch younger brother of University of Tennessee and NBA legend Bernard King and a player that Ungrady equates with the expectations of McMillen or Malone when it was first revealed he would be joining the Terps. As a senior at Fort Hamilton High School in Brooklyn, New York, King averaged 38.6 points and 22 rebounds per game after being featured in *Sports Illustrated* at only 15 and in a book by Rick Telander called *Heaven Is a Playground* at just 14 years of age. As Ungrady points out in *Legends of Maryland*, by the time he got to College Park, he had been rated among the best players ever produced by New York City's fertile basketball playgrounds.[194]

The credit for yet another No. 1 signing actually belonged to Harrington. "There's no other way to describe it. Joe did a great job on Albert," Driesell has stated. "When I finally got to one of Albert's high school games with Joe, the gym was so small, the free-throw line on one end served as the half court line on the other. They had to have police security at the games and only very select people got in. Albert got about 50 (points) that night."

Driesell, who was on crutches at the time with a torn Achilles tendon, knew that the University of Arizona (Lute Olson) was also "hot" on King's "trail" and as a result hoped to expedite his signing as quickly as possible. When just such a breakthrough occurred, he described it this way:

> His AAU coach was also a lawyer and he called to say "be in his office the next day and Albert would be there to sign." He then added, "don't tell anyone or he won't sign." So we kept everything under wraps and we were there on time, but Albert wasn't. In fact, he didn't get there until about an hour later, which really had us worried, but he finally arrived, signed, and had four great years (playing for Maryland).[195]

Joining King, the big city protégée, just one year later, was his small-town counterpart in terms of potential. It's just that not as many people knew about Buck Williams of Rocky Mount, North Carolina. In fact, at 6 feet, 8 inches, Williams came from a home so small (his father had built it) that he had to duck just to get through the doors. According to Driesell, North Carolina wasn't interested in Williams because they already had future All-American James Worthy committed and because the Tar Heel brain trust felt the Rocky Mount senior would need a year of prep school. Once again, Carolina's loss was "Lefty's" gain, however, and Williams and King would become among the most successful roommates in college basketball history before their days in College Park were done.[196]

At the same time, not all such Maryland recruiting ventures had turned out as well. One that got away that Driesell dearly wanted from right at his College Park doorstep was Adrian Dantley of local DeMatha High School, whose presence could have surely eradicated the previously alluded to "down years" of 1976–1978. Dantley would instead become a two-time All-American at Notre Dame and an NBA first-round draft pick (eventual Duke great Danny Ferry and North Carolina All-American J. R. Reid were two other ACC stars "Lefty" missed out on despite his best recruiting efforts).[197]

Nevertheless, between 1977–1978 and 1980–1981, the two major standouts he did land, King and Williams, would average 17.4 points and 6.1 rebounds and 13.6 points and a prodigious 10.9 rebounds, respectively, for their Maryland careers. Together they would lead the Terrapins to a 24–7 record and NCAA East Regional in 1979–1980 and a 21–10 mark and Mideast Regional in 1980–1981 with both earning All-American recognition (King twice, Williams once).[198] In fact, when they entered the NBA Draft together in 1981, the New Jersey Nets pulled off a coup by being able to land both in the first round. King would go on to play nine years in the NBA with New Jersey, Philadelphia, San Antonio, and Washington (Bullets), while Williams would last 17 with the Nets, Portland, and New York.[199] Like McMillen, Elmore, and Lucas before them, they would each have their Maryland jerseys retired.[200]

They were the major stars, but "Lefty" and his staff had accumulated plenty of other individual talent by the time the 1980s approached. Along with the returning Olympian, Sheppard, Greg Manning (who ironically would one day serve as Driesell's second athletic director at Georgia State University) was a slick-shooting, 6-foot, 1-inch guard; Ernie Graham was a tremendous offensive player at 6 feet, 7 inches, capable of big numbers in both points and assists; and 6-foot, 8-inch Lawrence Boston was good enough to average 15.5 points per game one season and just under eight rebounds a game for his four-year career. [201] "We were loaded with talent, but sometimes you can have too much," Manning has been quoted as saying in reference to the "class warfare" and "chemistry issues" that Driesell had to solve before his 1979–1980 team could live up to its NCAA Sweet 16 and No. 8 final ranking.[202]

Williams, who 7-foot, 4-inch Ralph Sampson, the University of Virginia's three-time national player of the year later called the toughest player he ever had to go against,[203] was a deeply religious young man despite what "Lefty" termed "a tough, aggressive, almost mean streak" on the court. "Buck and I were attending the same church in College Park, Berwyn Baptist, when he came up with the idea of a team retreat," Driesell remembered.

> Reverend Charlie Chilton was the pastor and with my approval, he and Buck set it up. But when they announced the dates, a lot of players started coming up with excuses why they couldn't go. That's when Buck said, "Coach, don't you worry about it, they will be there" and they were. After that, a lot of them started learning more about the Old and New Testaments and wanted to do it again. We continued until the NCAA said you couldn't engage in such team building activities anymore.[204]

A member of the 1980 U.S. Olympic team that did not get to compete due the Soviet invasion of Afghanistan and President Jimmy Carter's decision to boycott the Moscow Games as a result, Williams never forgot the encouragement he received from Driesell during his recruitment, especially the way he emphasized "I could make it if I just went to class."[205] Driesell, in turn, remained steadfastly supportive of Williams, even when faced with sending him against much bigger players. "I'm not worried about Buck," Driesell was often quoted as saying. "I guarantee you he's going to outplay just about everyone he goes up against."[206]

King, meanwhile, never seemed to quite live up to the enormous hype that preceded his arrival in College Park, but he admittedly felt more comfortable by the time his third season rolled around. "I think your personality on the court changes with your personality off the court and I started feeling more comfortable with my surroundings at the university from my junior season on," Ungrady quoted him as saying in *Legends*.[207] Nevertheless, when Maryland lost nine games his senior year, dropping from a preseason No. 4 ranking all the way to No. 20 and prompting boos from the usually supportive Terrapin fans, he openly criticized that reaction before taking the court for his final game at Cole Field House, a game he would ultimately take over with 28 points on 13 of 16 shooting from the field. It was a virtuoso performance that had the home crowd chanting "Albert! Albert!" before it was finally over, effectively erasing whatever bad taste might have otherwise lingered from his college days.[208]

"People would always say that I didn't like basketball or didn't want to talk about it," he would reiterate years afterward. "It was never that I didn't want to talk about it or didn't like it. I loved it. It obviously benefitted me and my family. It's just that I never wanted the stereotype of just being a jock." In radio voice Johnny Holliday's *Hoop Tales: Maryland Terrapins Men's Basketball*, he would add, "But I think back to Cole—coming through that tunnel—and how great the players and Coach 'Lefty' were. 'Lefty' was in a league by himself as far as personality was concerned. I probably helped him go bald, but it was all great fun."[209]

"Lefty" Driesell's grandfather and grandmother stand in the doorway of the F. Driesell & Son Jewelry Store along with his father as a little boy. Founded in 1883, it was the family business in Norfolk, Virginia, and the city's oldest jewelry store before it closed in the mid 1900s. Interested mainly in athletics while he was growing up, "Lefty" never showed any interest in managing or inheriting the store.

Courtesy Courtesy Charles G. Driesell

Just 18 months younger than her big brother, Martha Radcliffe remembered "Lefty" Driesell being a true "gym rat" during their formative years in Norfolk, Virginia. In fact, whenever discipline was required for him at a young age, she recalled their parents taking away his sports equipment.

Courtesy Martha Radcliffe

When he was in second grade, "Lefty" Driesell's family moved into this two-story house near Norfolk's Granby School, the home he would grow up in on the way to becoming a basketball legend. Today, the house is one of several properties that Driesell leases.

Photo by F. Martin Harmon

Despite an ear problem that conspired to limit his collegiate playing time, "Lefty" Driesell was a valuable backup at Duke University at a time when Blue Devil basketball was first becoming a national contender.

Courtesy Duke Sports Information

With "Lefty" Driesell (back row, second from left) as its All-State star, Granby High School would claim the 1950 Virginia State Basketball Championship. For Driesell it was just one part of a long Granby career that famously began with him serving as a grade school water boy for the high school athletic teams.

Courtesy Granby High School

After enduring a 9-14 finish in his first season as a college coach at Davidson, "Lefty" Driesell (back row on left) got things turned around in year two when his Wildcats finished 14-11. Among the varsity players that year was Terry Holland (back row, second from right), who had been Driesell's first recruit and who would succeed him as head coach eight years later.

Courtesy Davidson College Archives

Kneeling with his first big collegiate star, Fred Hetzel, in this Davidson College publicity photo, "Lefty" Driesell led the little private school in North Carolina to national prominence for the first time in the early 1960s, something Hetzel still considers among the most amazing college basketball feats ever.

Pictured during his Davidson years giving his Wildcats sideline instructions, "Lefty Driesell relied on a double-post, one-guard offense that got the ball inside and could run with the best teams in the country despite limited substitutions. He wanted his best five players on the court as much as possible.

Courtesy Davidson College Archives

A tremendous natural athlete also recruited as a quarterback for football by both Notre Dame and Ohio State University, Dick Snyder followed Fred Hetzel as "Lefty" Driesell's second All-American at Davidson College. The Ohio native went on to a 13-year NBA career.

Courtesy Davidson College Archives

Led by the first African-American player in Davidson College history, Mike Maloy (second from right), "Lefty" Driesell's nationally ranked Wildcats would capture the Southern Conference championship in 1968 and 1969 and advance to the NCAA East Regional Finals both years.

Courtesy Davidson College Archives

Seated on the edge of his desk in his office at the University of Maryland, "Lefty" Driesell brought a new attitude to the Terrapins and a new way of competing with the best teams in the tough Atlantic Coast Conference. Upgraded facilities and an improved home court atmosphere were among the things he wanted upon becoming the Terps new head coach in 1969.

Courtesy Maryland Athletics

After connecting on a game-winning shot in 1971, Jim O'Brien is carried off the Cole Fieldhouse floor on the shoulders of exultant University of Maryland students. As indicated by the scoreboard, it was an extremely low scoring, one-point victory (31-30) over a heavily favored University of South Carolina team and the first big truly win for "Lefty" Driesell at UM.

Courtesy Maryland Athletics

Embellishing his reputation as a great recruiter was "Lefty" Driesell's dual
signing of Len Elmore and Tom McMillen for the University of Maryland,
two of the nation's most heralded prospects. Together they would give the
Terps one of the most talented frontcourts in the country during the early
1970s and lead the way to new heights (and expectations) in the Atlantic
Coast Conference.

Courtesy Maryland Athletics

With head coach "Lefty" Driesell (in dark sneakers), assistant coach George Raveling, and sports information director Jack Zane manning stop watches at the track finish line, the first ever Midnight Madness practice was staged outdoors at the University of Maryland on October 5, 1971. The timed mile run was how Driesell always opened his first practice and the midnight start was designed to give him a jump on the competition.

Courtesy Maryland Athletics

Pictured alongside the scorer's table while providing his team encouragement, "Lefty" Driesell became synonymous with the University of Maryland's Cole Fieldhouse, where he had the seats moved closer to the court and enjoyed a tremendous home court winning percentage. For a while, he even entered Cole before games to the triumphant musical strains of "Hail to the Chief."

Courtesy Maryland Athletics

A smile on his face, "Lefty" Driesell enjoyed his years at the University of Maryland, which he built into a national power before being made a scapegoat in the aftermath of the Len Bias' tragedy. This headshot was obviously taken during earlier, happier times at College Park.

Courtesy Maryland Athletics

"Lefty" Driesell was named the new head coach at James Madison University in 1988, two years after he relinquished the same duties at the University of Maryland following 17 seasons as head coach of the Terps. Hundreds were on hand for this press conference at the JMU Convocation Center.

Courtesy JMU Athletics Communications

Photographed on the sidelines together during the heat of a game at James Madison University, "Lefty" Driesell was glad to have his son, Chuck Driesell (lower right), as part of his staff at JMU. The younger Driesell had also played for his father at Maryland.

At Georgia State University, "Lefty" Driesell's first coaching staff included Schuyler Pindar, Scott Adubato, Phil Cunningham, and Michael Perry. Missing was Chuck Driesell, who he had hoped to bring with him from his staff at James Madison before being barred from doing by State of Georgia nepotism guidelines.

Courtesy Georgia State University Sports Communications

Moments after earning his 700th win at the start of the 1998-99 season, "Lefty" Driesell was presented with a game ball emblematic of yet another career milestone by Georgia State Athletic Director Orby Moss (left) and Panther Public Address Announcer Rob Preiditsch.

Courtesy Georgia State University Sports Communications

Throughout his 41-year coaching career, "Lefty" Driesell could be counted on for engaging television interviews, including this one near the end of his career. Only once, however, did he take on the now common role of former coach turned TV analyst – when he assisted on Atlantic Coast Conference Games of the Week after resigning as coach at the University of Maryland in 1986.

Courtesy Georgia State University Sports Communications

Throughout his coaching career, "Lefty" Driesell was blessed with out-standing individual performers, including future pros like Albert King, shown here years after starring for The Lefthander at the University of Maryland. When he signed with the Terps out of Brooklyn, New York, King was among the most acclaimed recruits ever.

Courtesy Georgia State University Sports Communications

Perhaps the biggest coaching disappointment ever for "Lefty" Driesell was when Moses Malone, one of the game's future greats, went from heralded University of Maryland recruit to one of the first high school stars ever to go straight to the pros when he signed with the ABA Utah Stars in 1974. Nevertheless, they have remained close friends ever since as illustrated by this picture.

Courtesy Georgia State University Sports Communications

Together, Shenard Long, a transfer from Georgetown University, and "Lefty" Driesell would lead Georgia State University to its greatest basketball achievements ever in 2001 as Trans America Athletic Conference Player and Coach of the Year.

Courtesy Georgia State University Sports Communications

After cutting down the nets at the 2001 Trans America Conference Tournament, "Lefty" Driesell gives a "V for victory" sign to Georgia State supporters. It was his 21st and final conference championship. His Panthers would advance to the NCAA Tournament and his career best 29th win in a single season.

Courtesy Georgia State University Sports Communications

Kevin Morris, a transfer from Georgia Tech who joined "Lefty" Driesell at Georgia State University after he took over Atlanta's "other" Division I program, exemplified the sheer joy of a 2001 NCAA Tournament milestone in this photo, taken seconds after the final buzzer in the Panthers' first round upset of Big 10 power Wisconsin. Ironically, GSU would lose in the second round to Maryland.

Courtesy Georgia State University Sports Communications

Among those on hand for The Old Lefthander's induction into the National Collegiate Basketball Hall of Fame were two of his early mainstays at the University of Maryland, longtime assistant coach Joe Harrington (left) and three-time All-American Tom McMillen (center). Together again, they formed a happy trio in Kansas City.

Courtesy Georgia State University Sports Communications

A member of the Class of 2007, "Lefty" Driesell was inducted into the
Collegiate Basketball Hall of Fame in Kansas City, where he joined other
coaching legends like Henry Iba and John McClendon. He's shown here
during his acceptance speech.

Courtesy Georgia State University Sports Communications

Called "the greatest program builder ever in college basketball," by longtime TV analyst Billy Packer, "Lefty" Driesell has always enjoyed good
relations with the game's other luminaries. He's shown here with Packer
(seated) and fellow college basketball commentator Dick Vitale (center).

Courtesy Georgia State University Sports Communications

After finally retiring from coaching in 2003, "Lefty" and Joyce Driesell returned to their roots in the Norfolk, Virginia area by moving into a fourth floor condo within easy sight of surf and sand at Virginia Beach.

Photo by F. Martin Harmon

Still in love with the game that's been so much a part of his life, "Lefty" Driesell continues to attend college basketball games into his '80s – and as this picture indicates, he gets into the action now as much as ever.

Courtesy Georgia State University Sports Communications

Over 60 years after earning the trophy he holds, emblematic of Norfolk, Virginia's outstanding prep player in 1950, "Lefty" Driesell returned to the Granby High School campus for this picture—the school he starred at as a player and the place where he began his legendary coaching career in 1955.

Photo by F. Martin Harmon

11

Rebuilding with Local Stars

Actually, "Lefty" would have probably sympathized with any of his players feeling stereotyped. As we have seen, while big-name recruits were obviously part of his resume at Davidson and Maryland, the reputation of great recruiter as opposed to great coach gradually became the label most identified with his legacy, a reputation he would work to refute time and time again, especially in his final five seasons at Maryland and later at two other more remote outposts of college basketball.

As McMullen emphasized in *Maryland Basketball*, his response to critics after a much-needed road win late in the 1980–1981 season was a simple, "I can coach," a line that was liberally replayed by the media when Maryland romped over Sampson and Virginia, 85–62, in that year's ACC Tournament Semifinals.[210] Unfortunately with pressure mounting, the renewed incentive sparked by such criticism was not enough to help the Terps overcome their ongoing ACC tourney misfortunes, as they suffered their fifth ACC Finals loss in a decade, a 61–60 heartbreaker to North Carolina. That prompted Driesell to remark at the time, "I'm a religious man and I don't think the Lord wants me to win this thing."[211]

According to *Maryland Basketball*, once again, "With Ernie Graham, Albert King, Greg Manning, and Buck Williams moving on, Driesell was in desperate need of some offense in 1981–1982."[212] Where he looked to replace it was locally. Joining the Terrapin program would be a slinky, left-handed freshman from nearby DeMatha, one of those who didn't get away who would average over 15 points per game in his first year and score over 2,000 points in his college career. In fact, Adrian Branch was one of the first of a new breed of player in the college game, a mobile 6-foot, 8-inch star with enough ball-handling skills to overpower at guard and enough size plus quickness to also flourish at forward, a true guard/forward. While never the consummate playmaking big guard of the Oscar Robertson, "Magic" Johnson mold, Branch nevertheless could go one-on-one against smaller, quicker players or use his mobility skills to best advantage in a fast-paced game versus bigger, slower opponents. He was truly a type of player Driesell had not had before.

Branch was a bright spot in a 16–13 year, the first following the dynamic duo of King and Williams.[213] Also on that team was Driesell's son, Chuck, a 6-foot, 2-inch guard who had prepped in nearby Silver Spring, Maryland. As previously noted, like father, like son, Chuck would eventually go on to coach college basketball, including a stint as an assistant at Maryland and his first Division I head job (The Citadel) in the same Southern Conference where "Lefty" got his start.[214] Another new and relatively local contributor on that team was Jeff Adkins of Martinsville, Virginia. Waiting in the wings, however, was the best local product of Driesell's Maryland tenure, a player with so much natural ability and potential that he would be one of the very few rightful players to be allowed in the same breath as basketball's recognized all-time best, Michael Jordan.[215] Closer even than DeMatha, which is little more than two miles away from the Maryland campus, is Northwestern High School, the launching site for Len Bias. As McMullen pointed out, he could walk from his high school gym to Cole (Field House) in just 20 minutes.[216]

In fact, as different and removed as the New York big-city and North Carolina small-town backgrounds of his two outgoing stars, King and Williams, had been, the close proximity of the two players who would become Driesell's last major Maryland combo, Branch and Bias, seemed almost too familiar and perfect to be true. What college coach doesn't dream of having great players from his university's immediate area? What better way to ensure local interest, ticket sales, and financial support? In Branch and one year later Bias, "Lefty" recruited made-in-Maryland star power, the kind that would translate into attendance resurgence and renewed ACC success.[217]

For his part, Bias was a muscular, 6-foot, 8-inch missile with touch. Although not the ball-handling revelation of later, similar-sized (and "abilitied") basketball prodigies like LeBron James, Bias was nonetheless a great jump shooter and shot blocker who could (and did) constantly elevate over and excel against much bigger or better hyped players throughout his college career. No less an ACC authority than Duke's esteemed Mike Kryzewski, the winningest men's coach of all time, once called he and Jordan the most gifted players he had seen in all his years in the league and Bias would outpoint, outrebound, and out-draft-pick *magnificent Mike* (he was the NBA's second overall pick two years after Jordan was the third) in their final collegiate seasons.[218] In fact, Bias posted steadily improving numbers at Maryland throughout his four college seasons, finishing third to Branch's fifth in career scoring and exactly matching his 16.4 points per game four-year average. *Washington Post* and ESPN analyst Michael Wilbon even said, "I saw great players from the ACC and Big East every night. Jordan, (Patrick) Ewing, (Chris) Mullin, Sampson. Later on David Robinson. But Len Bias was the most awesome collegiate player of that bunch. (His) jumper was so pure. I mean, Michael Jordan, at that time, would have killed for that jumper. And Bias was two inches taller."[219]

But while sheer natural ability is what would be remembered about Bias, the uniqueness of Branch is what would ensure his legacy and make for some very memorable moments even before Bias arrived on the scene. One of those would occur at the end of Branch's freshman season. The Terps had lost four ACC games in a row with Sampson and No. 1 ranked Virginia next up in the final home game at Cole. Admittedly, even the most loyal fans didn't give Maryland much chance that night, but Driesell had by then seen enough of his talented, local freshman to conjure up a nothing-to-lose plan that he thought just might produce one of the season's major upsets…and it did.

"I didn't think we could beat Virginia just by running with them," he has reminisced many times since.

> Adrian was a great one-on-one player and we ran this play called Drop. We would just give him the ball in middle court and everybody else set up on the baseline, with the two inside guys as potential rebounders in case he missed. I didn't think Virginia had anyone that could guard Adrian (man-to-man) and I was right. They never went to a zone defense and they never stopped him. So we just played one-on-one with Adrian the whole game. I think we were probably the first team to ever do something like that. We also employed a defense against Sampson that I called Special that was like a triangle and two, and we were the only team to beat Virginia during that regular season (47–46 in overtime).[220]

Branch would score on 12 of his 16 field goal attempts and five of six free throws for 29 of the Terrapins' 47 points and although he had made big shots in many other games, none was bigger than his 15-footer from the foul line as time expired against the top ranked Cavaliers. Many still consider it one of the greatest individual performances in Terp history, but it should also rank as one of their greatest game plans (translation: great coaching) as well.[221]

In 1982–1983, Branch assumed even more leadership, averaging a career high 18.7 points per contest, on a squad with size throughout. Along with the 6-foot, 8-inch Branch, Adkins was a big point guard at 6 feet, 5 inches who started all 30 games and led the Terps in assists, and additional leading roles were played by 6-foot, 9-inch, 220-pound Ben Coleman; 6-foot, 6-inch, 220-pound defensive ace Herman Veal; and 6-foot, 9-inch, 220-pound Mark Fothergill, a mix-and-match trio from all over the map (Coleman, Minneapolis, Minnesota; Veal, Jackson, Mississippi; and Fothergill, Somerset, Kentucky). Together they would outrebound and outshoot their opponents from the field to accomplish a 20–10 mark and second-round finish at the NCAA Midwest Regional. As just a freshman, the still budding Bias was also in that mix, averaging 7.1 points in spot relief of his more experienced teammates and hitting the winning jumper in a first round win at the NCAA Tournament—an early portent of the brilliance to come.[222] Paul Baker, an overseer of ACC officials who attended games at Maryland from 1981 through 1989, issued the following recollection in McMullen's book, "He had not been that highly recruited. Bias had been nasty and abusive at a summer camp, and instead of having college coaches come to him, he repelled them. He was still a diamond in the rough his freshman year."[223]

His promise, however, would really begin to surface in 1983–1984, as Bias and Coleman both averaged over 15 points per game, leading the way to Driesell's long-awaited ACC

Tournament Championship and NCAA Sweet 16 finish. Without the need to score as much, Branch averaged 13 per contest and both Adkins and Veal were usually close to double figures as well with 9.8 and 8.4 averages, respectively. There was also a new face in the Terps' championship mix, North Carolinian Keith Gatlin, another slick, 6-foot, 5-inch point guard who had turned down other ACC suitors and who would take over much of the playmaking as a freshman. "When his sophomore season began, the light wasn't on in Lenny's head yet, but you could see he was going to be a megastar," Gatlin remembered of Bias. "You could tell he had the talent, that it was going to be his team and he was going to be the man. In the second half of that season, he did more than just take his game to another level, he went to another planet."[224]

Number 8 in the preseason rankings that year, there was considerable buzz surrounding Driesell's quintet when it opened the ACC with wins over No. 6 Boston College and its future Maryland Coach Gary Williams, and defending NCAA champion North Carolina State, a surprise winner over heavily favored Houston in the NCAA Finals the year before. Coleman was still around and Bias was really coming on, and the team still bore what McMullen termed "Branch's stamp" until trouble struck in late January. That's when both Branch and reserve guard Steve Rivers were charged with possession of marijuana and suspended. Branch, however, received "probation before judgment" and rejoined the team two weeks later. In his absence, the Terps had dropped a pair of double overtime decisions and before chemistry with his teammates could be re-established; they also lost a rare home game to Duke.[225]

When the three-game slide finally ended, it was Bias and Gatlin who would propel the Terps back into the ACC race and the tournament's second seed. Led by Jordan, the University of North Carolina was undefeated and the overwhelming favorite as the conference tourney began, but once again Driesell coached the Terps past N.C. State's defending national champs in the first round, utilized his superior balance to beat Wake Forest in the semis, and then instituted to a 2–3 zone defense at halftime of the finals against Duke (upset winner over its arch rival UNC the night before), a move that would completely stymie the Blue Devils' main star at the time, Johnny Dawkins. At the same time, Bias was really coming of age with 26 points versus Duke (at that time a career high) and he would go on to be the unanimous tournament MVP. After finally winning the tournament, Driesell famously promised to attach the trophy to the hood of his car and drive all over the state of North Carolina, but his elation was short lived at the NCAA, where Maryland ultimately lost to Illinois in the Mideast Regional.[226]

Meanwhile, the legend of Len Bias was growing. His scoring average jumped almost four whole points to 18.9 per game and he became the first Maryland player to earn ACC Player of the Year honors as a junior, setting himself up to become the only Terrapin to earn that recognition in back-to-back seasons. At the same time, Branch was also averaging over 18 points per game as a senior, the only time two Terrapins have both averaged that much in a single season, and once again they enjoyed an outstanding campaign, finishing 25–12 and advancing to the NCAA Southeast Regional Semifinal.[227] Along the way, Driesell added his 500th career victory, celebrated by what would be the first of several career milestone basketballs to adorn his office in the years ahead.[228]

Despite their dual threat and combined production, McMullen spoke of the combination of Branch and Bias as "an uneasy alliance," for three seasons. But Branch (who like Len Elmore before him would go on to a second basketball career as an analyst) looked to diffuse such comments with statements like, "It's not where you've been, it's where you're going. It's how you finish." He picked "Lefty" and Maryland over coaches like Dean Smith and North Carolina primarily to play close to home. He led all ACC freshmen in scoring, including Michael Jordan, and he earned Driesell's respect quickly as indicated by "Lefty" linking Branch and Lucas, ironically his two outstanding lefthanders, as the two best freshmen he ever coached.[229] "I loved my coach, worked hard, and was happy I went there," Branch more recently recalled.[230] Selected in the NBA Draft's second round by Chicago, he left the College Park spotlight to a single player like never before.[231] Bias was that player, but unfortunately, unlike Branch, his spotlight would never go away.

12

The Bias Saga

Undeserved, Unforgiving, Unending

"Everybody loved Len," Adrian Branch was quoted as saying in *Legends of Maryland Basketball*. And in 1985–1986, it seemed every college basketball fan and evaluator really did love Len Bias as he exploded up the charts his senior season. After nearly turning pro following his junior year, his decision to remain at Maryland turned to gold when he was named ACC Player of the Year and All-American for the second straight season while also becoming the Terrapins all-time scoring leader (since passed by Juan Dixon, 1999–2002, and Greivias Vasquez, 2006–2010).[232]

It truly seemed everyone connected to the game was in awe of Len Bias, especially those living in the Baltimore-Washington, D.C. area. Walt Williams was one of several future, local stars who would sign with Maryland because of Bias's magnetism. He had been in awe just to step on the court with his idol, which he once did during a pickup game as a 14-year-old. "I was a very big Len Bias fan. It was a big thing for me to go to Maryland and follow in his footsteps," the future All-American and finalist for Wooden and Naismith Player of the Year honors confessed years later in *Legends of Maryland Basketball*.[233] Another, equally smitten, future Terp was Keith Booth. According to Dave Ungrady in *Born Ready*, Booth "talked excitedly about the day he met Bias, his hero," as a 10-

year-old and remembered him as the player he "fell in love with growing up."[234]

That kind of magnetism was already building when Bias led Maryland to the Sweet 16 the year before, but the early part of 1985–1986 would prove a struggle for the Terrapins and their superstar, one of only two seniors on an otherwise inexperienced team. Ranked 17th when they lost to unranked Ohio State in the third game of the season, the Terps failed to achieve a national ranking the remainder of the year. With an NCAA bid tenuous, Driesell estimated Maryland would need to win three of its final four regular season games to reach the proverbial *Big Dance*.[235] That's when more of Bias's heroics kicked in, as his 35 points propelled the Terps to a shocking 77–72 victory at North Carolina in overtime, a performance that Driesell called the best he had ever seen and a game that prompted *Washington Post* columnist Thomas Boswell to label Bias "The Answer."[236] The Terps would go on to finish with easy wins at Wake Forest (59–48) and in the regular season finale against Virginia (87–72) to continue "Lefty's" four-year run of consecutive NCAA Tournament appearances and sixth over his final seven seasons at College Park. Bias would finish with a sensational 23.2 per game point average and shoot almost 55 percent from the field as a senior.[237]

Despite the great statistics, however, media representatives covering Maryland recalled what they perceived as problems in his personality. At least one of them, Molly Durham of the *Baltimore Evening Sun,* reportedly considered Bias "manipulative" and, according to Fraser Smith's book, his "macho image made his insecurities more intense."[238] John Hawkins of the *Baltimore News American* even termed him "one of the biggest jerks" he ever dealt with. "It's terrible to say, but he was the surliest, the most uncooperative of all the players,"

Hawkins was quoted as saying. "(But) no one was going to write that Len Bias was a jerk—because he was an All-American."[239]

Driesell, meanwhile, was never a party to such behind-the-scenes negativity when it came to his last Terrapin star; never accepted published reports of personal shortcomings that surfaced after his tragic death; and still doesn't permit rumors, innuendo, or even factual illegalities to creep into conversation about Bias and what happened before or since that fateful night. All "Lefty" ever saw (or still sees) in Len Bias was the positive. Watching him mature into a truly great player, The Lefthander believed, along with everyone else, that he was destined for a tremendous professional career, especially when his good friend "Red" Auerbach moved up to acquire him for the Celtics with the second pick in the 1986 NBA Draft.

"The last time we spoke was when he called me from the draft to say, 'Coach, thank you for everything you did for me. I wouldn't be here without you,'" Driesell remembered before adding, "He was a great Christian, a great kid, and he came from a good background. I would have bet my life he never used drugs. I even knew of times when people tried to get him to have a beer and he wouldn't do it. He would have been the last one on that team that I would have suspected."[240]

Those remain remarkable words after all these years by someone whose career (and life) was unalterably changed by the person of whom he spoke. Perhaps Driesell's retelling of events as he remembered them could put such time-tested loyalty into perspective. If nothing else, it seemed to make sense in the context of what happened next…and since. "I have always remembered going to bed that night after the draft feeling really good about Len and the prestige such a high draft choice was going to give our program," Driesell, in his own words, reluctantly began.

> About 7 a.m. the next morning I went to the Springbrook High School track (only a block away) for a jog before returning to the house for a shower and some breakfast. It was while I was eating breakfast that the phone rang. It was a nurse at the hospital. After identifying myself, she asked if any of my players were allergic to any drugs. I told her I wasn't sure and I gave her the number for our team trainer, J. J. Bush. About 30 minutes later, right before I left for the office, she called back and told me that Len's parents were there at the hospital and they wanted me to come over there right away. When I got there, I found them sitting in a little waiting room and that's when I first learned that he was dead of an apparent heart attack.

Obviously still painful to remember after all the years, Driesell continued,

> They had him on a respirator, but by the time I got there, they had taken it off. I went in to see him and they had him on an examining table. There was blood all over his face. I remained there about an hour. Other players were there and I was trying to calm them, but I was in shock, too. None of us hardly knew where we were or what we were doing. I couldn't believe it and neither could they. There was nothing I could do but try and console my players. When I finally left, I drove straight to the office. It's a wonder I was able to get there. It was a weekday, so both secretaries and all my assistant coaches were in the office. When I walked in, they already knew. It was all over the radio. I went straight into (assistant) Oliver Purnell's office, which was near the front, and called "Red" (Auerbach). When I told him what had happened, he just about dropped the phone and then I remember him saying "No, no, he was just here. It can't be true. What happened? What Happened?"[241]

What happened next would come back to haunt Driesell in the weeks and months ahead in ways obviously not considered at such a time of unfathomable loss. After hanging up with Auer-bach, he also spoke with Lee Fentress, Bias's agent and his own lawyer, by telephone. After informing him of the tragedy, he remembered Fentress saying, "They've got to rush him to Georgetown for a heart transplant." But after affirming it was too late for anything like that, "Lefty" recalled answering his next, obvious "what happened" question this way: "The players said he was messing around with some drugs and passed out," which prompted Fentress to come back with what Driesell has always remembered as, "Get a manager or an assistant coach over there (the dormitory) to clean up the room."[242]

What exactly was meant by that statement remains debatable almost 30 years later, but taken at face value and coming from a lawyer, it sounds as ill-advised now as it did then. Unfortunately, given his state of mind at the time, Driesell understandably didn't take time to think about how it sounded. "As I said, I was in Oliver's office and he was my top assistant," he reminded,

> so I just turned away from the phone and told Oliver what Lee (as a lawyer) said and he responded okay and that he would take our grad assistant, Jeff Atkins, with him. So Oliver and Jeff took off. By that time, the press and everybody else was arriving at the office and I knew I wasn't in any shape to talk with them, so I told the secretaries to hold my calls, went straight to my own office, and closed the door. I wanted to be alone, but that's when I got to thinking about what I had just told Oliver and how they really didn't need to be touching anything. Of course, those were pre-cell phone days, so there was really no way I could tell them anything else at that point. Luckily, when they got there, the

police were already there. He and Jeff didn't even go inside.[243]

Next, Driesell had all the players come to his house. "When they got over there, I was relieved to learn that Oliver hadn't done anything and we were all just trying to calm down. I assured them Len was a born-again Christian. I kept telling them not to worry about Leonard because, 'I know he's in heaven.'" Two policemen had already been to "Lefty's" house before the players arrived and once they got there they all wanted to know what they should say or do if questioned by police. Once again, Driesell sought Fentress's council for such advice. "Lee told me if they were his sons, he would tell them not to say anything to the police," he related, still relying on his attorney.[244]

Eventually, however, the fact Fentress was not a criminal attorney led Driesell to contact Edward Bennett Williams—yes, the same Edward Bennett Williams who once owned the Baltimore Orioles and was part owner of the Washington Redskins, and one of the best-known criminal lawyers in the country. After agreeing to take him on as a client, the first thing Williams instructed him to do was to say nothing to anyone, especially the press. That instruction also included Maryland Attorney General Bud Marshall, a politician up for re-election in 1986 and someone Driesell came to believe was determined to make a name for himself by cleaning up "the whole University of Maryland drug problem." According to "Lefty," Williams told him he would have to testify before the grand jury and coached him in that regard.[245]

Like Bias's funeral, the trial became a cause celeb with people like Jackson and Al Sharpton involved. "I was tried in the court of public opinion before I ever got to the court of law," Driesell remembered.

It was in the newspapers every day. It all started in the middle of the summer and it was October before I was finally called to testify. I even got questions like whether or not I had ever put players back on the bus after a road loss without feeding them. Without stooping to directly answer that question, I reminded everyone how well fed our players always were at every pregame meal.[246]

Ultimately, the idea of "Lefty" wanting "the room cleaned up," is what the State's case zeroed in on. Although never knowing for sure who shared this comment with investigators (despite long held suspicions), Driesell was able to shift fault for that initial (and unlawful sounding) instruction to Fentress, who was brought up on charges to disbar, but who also escaped penalty. "I was only repeating what the lawyer said. I never knew what he (Fentress) told the grand jury, but that's what I told them," Driesell confirmed.[247] According to a *Boston Herald* column headlined "Well-Deserved Victory for 'Lefty'" and dated 28 August 1986, jurors (in clearing him of obstruction charges) had drawn "a clear and correct distinction between an act of compassion and an act of corruption."[248] In *The Man to See*, a 1991 biography on Williams by Evan Thomas, the master attorney reputedly indicated the same thing in a less refined way when queried during the trial. That's when, upon the aftermath of Driesell's testimony, he admitted his client had done a "stupid thing" before adding, "but you can be stupid without being criminal."[249]

As for his still-maintained reasoning that he was simply giving Fentress's lawyerly instruction to Purnell that awful, blur-of-a-day, Driesell reaffirmed, "I would state on a stack of bibles to the present day that it never crossed my mind to cover something up. I've always said I would be glad to take a lie detector test to prove my sincerity about that."[250] Driesell spoke publicly about the case for the first time to *Sports Illustrated* following the trial in November 1986. Fentress confirmed his account in later news reports, while also alleging, according to the *SI* story, that "his offhand remark to clean the room" had come "at an emotional moment" for him as well "and without consideration of the implications."[251]

Regardless, the grand jury proceedings were only the start of "Lefty's" troubles. Ungrady made the point that "During the immediate months that followed Bias's death, Driesell must have felt he was living in a hell on earth. His reputation as a pioneer among college basketball coaches was transformed into one of a coach who was, at worst, indifferent to his athletes' academic needs, and, at best, blind to their off-court shenanigans." Among those who would later attest to Driesell's being unfairly made a scapegoat was Bush, the same athletic trainer who had been assigned to the team since 1971 and who, undoubtedly, was a close observer of the internally initiated university drama taking place at the time. "I think the buck should have stopped with Lenny (Bias)," Bush emphasized to Ungrady.[252]

But stop with Lenny it most certainly did not. According to Driesell, Maryland Chancellor John Slaughter, a nationally prominent African-American administrator who had been vice president and provost at Washington State University and director of Washington's National Science Foundation before assuming leadership at College Park in 1980, had been a basketball backer at Maryland during his early years on the job and even supported "Lefty's" 10-year contract extension, raise, and tenured status in 1984, a nearly $1 million total package.[253] That all changed with Bias's death, however, as Slaughter launched inquiries into the university's policies on drug and alcohol abuse, as well as the academic progress of all Terrapin athletes. Particular focus was given to Maryland men's basketball and football, obviously the highest profile programs, with Driesell and equally successful gridiron coach Bobby Ross at the respective helms.[254]

A year before Bias's death, one of the basketball team's academic advisers had quit over a dispute with Driesell and submitted a letter suggesting the athletic department was serving basketball but not academics, something that found its way to area newspapers.[255] This prior happening became magnified after his death when family members and at least one dissatisfied player questioned the coaching staff's (and by association the university's) commitment to academic progress,[256] and again when yet another academic advisor left the program, complaining to the *Washington Post* about players missing 35 to 40 percent of their classes during the season.[257] In days immediately following his death, James Bias, Len's father, also told the *Post* that UM exploited its athletes by suggesting they take easy courses and emphasizing athletics over academics.[258] It was even emphasized that Bias had not been attending class for several weeks despite being 21 hours short of graduation (although knowledge of his draft status and immediate earning potential seemed to render such *uncommon sense* charges irrelevant). Bias's own meeting with an academic coordinator about a week before his death was testament to why the coach remained confident the player truly wanted a degree and would have eventually completed all necessary course work after initiation of his professional career.[259]

It was all symptomatic of the cloud of scrutiny that enveloped the entire athletic program, a cloud the university administration never seemed intent on totally dispelling. Instead of banding together in a united way of facing the impending public relations storm, as might have happened under the best of working relationships following a tragedy, university leadership actually came across as accepting of the ratcheting investigation, especially when it led to examination of more intrinsic value to their own concerns, namely academics. "It was a terrible accident, but I think it got terribly screwed up because of a lack of leadership," Driesell has maintained. "I loved Leonard. He was loved by the whole community. I loved all my players like my own children. I remain proud of my 17 years at Maryland."[260]

13

"Bearing the Blame" for All

On 29 October 1986, in a poignant press conference that has been described many times, Charles "Lefty" Driesell resigned as head basketball coach at the University of Maryland. Never one to hide his feelings, characteristic of the genuine demeanor mentioned at the very beginning of this book, he was not a happy man when he exited Cole Field House that day.[261] Ultimately, he did what he had to do for the well-being of his family and the school. As for the basketball program he had built into a national contender, it would take years to recover and affect the lives of everyone involved.[262]

At the time and ever since, he has been painted as the classic scapegoat. *Webster's* describes such a person as "bearing the blame for others."[263] In Driesell's case, it would probably be more accurate if it read "bearing the blame for all" because if anyone, other than the adult perpetrator of the unlawful act of using drugs and accidentally taking one's own life, is to blame, then everyone in that person's life must share in the responsibility, including parents, siblings, girlfriends, friends, mentors, teachers, teammates, and yes, coaches.

Along with "Lefty," everyone mourned the loss and needed time to recover, but society's need to place blame along with other agendas conspired to set things in motion that gradually gained inexplicable momentum, leading to his resignation, the program's demise, angered allegiances, and finally NCAA probation for his successor, Bob Wade.[264] Although it may have seemed unlikely at the time, Driesell would coach again at two other Division I programs in need of his services, but, as we have seen, the stigma of that day (and time) would never go away. So much so, in fact, that if American Sport had its own unique reference guide, the definition of scapegoat might even carry the notation: *"see Charles Grice Driesell."*

"Lefty" was never accused of violating NCAA rules. In fact, Bob James, ACC commissioner for 16 years, affirmed as much at that time when he publicly stated, "I never heard so much as a rumor about 'Lefty' Driesell breaking—or even bending—a rule."[265] Just as the grand jury found nothing wrong with the coach's actions from a legal standpoint, so too there was nothing Slaughter's administration could use as a basis for voiding his contract because of a rules violation.[266] Instead, it was the team's academic progress they targeted as sufficient cause to make a basketball coaching change. In Ungrady's book, David Dickerson, a freshman when Bias died and later a Driesell assistant at James Madison, defended "Lefty's" approach to academics by stating, "Coach Driesell has been vilified, but he was very in tune with his players' academic success and he wanted his players to be successful (students). I never saw or heard him put academics on the back burner and I never saw him sacrifice a kid's academic progress for athletic gain." Sue Tyler, a coach and associate athletic director at Maryland for 20 years, even recalled the way he pressured assistant coaches to always make sure players were attending classes. "We've got to get their butts to class," she remembered him telling them on more than one occasion. Phil Nevin, an infrequently used 6-foot, 11-inch backup, even commented about the change when Wade took over by stating, "'Lefty' treated us like adults. After (the Bias tragedy), they treated us like children. They checked your schoolwork and had people checking on us every other day. Wade tried to run your life."[267]

As for his own defense, Driesell went to great lengths in the months following Bias's death to refute such charges through detailed correspondence. In the first such communication sent directly to Slaughter, a memo dated 11 August 1986, he addressed a chart the administration had apparently compiled for a meeting showing athletic graduation data from 1975 through 1979. Among his main points: the men's basketball team's graduation rate exceeded the overall university's male graduation rate for the same period; the team graduation percentage was low because it unfairly penalized his squad for seven players who transferred to other colleges and one who died (besides Bias); and because two of his players from that period (Albert King and Buck Williams) had turned pro early, the listed percentage was again lower than it should have been.[268] Based on this information and common sense, he has always maintained his teams' graduation percentage was much better than what was being cited by the university at that time.

Less than a month later in a letter dated 4 September 1986, he again addressed the issues mounting against him. These included Bias's academic standing at the time of his death, which would have been easily rectified by his intention to make up any hours he needed to graduate at summer school; his conduct following Bias's death made mute by his being absolved of any wrong doing by the grand jury; recriminations against him due to accusations of drug use by Terrapin basketball players, something he termed "baseless" and "ironic" given his prior support of Maryland becoming one of only two ACC athletic departments with active drug testing at the time; and the academic success rate of his players, which he refuted with an overall graduation rate through 31 years of coaching that was better than his overall winning percentage, and a graduation rate for basketball playing black males at Maryland that was much higher than for other African Americans at the university.[269]

Finally, on 16 September 1986, he wrote to Slaughter one last time in reference to a meeting they apparently had four days earlier. Its opening paragraphs included the unequivocal statement:

> I want to state in writing that there is no foundation whatsoever to the accusation that I received a "kickback" as a result of Leonard Bias's selection of Mr. Lee Fentress as his agent and attorney. I have never been offered any kind of monetary reward for "delivering" a player and I would never accept one. In fact, if any attorney or agent proposed such an arrangement, I would do everything in my power to discourage the player concerned from having anything to do with that person. I am very upset that a charge of this kind should be leveled against me.[270]

By that time, it must have been fairly obvious that a witch hunt was underway and that Maryland's chancellor had decided his men's basketball coach had to go. Ungrady makes note of "Driesell's public campaign to preserve his integrity and save his job" and stated, "Through all the scrutiny, Driesell remained defiant."[271] Defiance, however, was not about to change Slaughter's mind. Some have equated that with his desire to name the ACC's first black head coach, which Wade, a local coaching legend at Dunbar High School in Baltimore and someone Driesell had not gotten along with, would become once "Lefty" was gone.[272]

Meanwhile, "Lefty's" new attorney, Williams, was negotiating behind the scenes to resolve the administration's obvious intent with his client's desires and remaining nine-year contract. "Slaughter first wanted me to coach one more year and then retire," Driesell remembered. "He thought he was going to clean everything up and change academics at the University of Maryland. He wouldn't let me respond to the Board of Regents about things he was telling them."[273]

At his final presentation to "Lefty," Williams painted the following scenario: "He said, "Lefty,' we can take them to court and you would win, but it would take a long time and in the process you would spend more on legal fees than your contract is worth,'" Driesell remembered. "'What you can take from this is nine years left on your contract at $90,000 per year, plus $50,000 the first year for what would have been your (coach's) TV show, and free access to the university athletic facilities for five years to run your camps,' which was worth between $20,000 and $30,000 a year," he continued. "I already had tenure, so they proposed an assistant AD position over sports information and marketing with a separate office and secretary. I wouldn't have any out of state travel—basically just show up and get paid."[274]

The only other stipulation to the deal was that "Lefty" couldn't say anything bad about the University of Maryland for the duration of the contract. "It set me up into my 60s," he said. "It was take this or take 'em to court, according to Williams, and I had already gotten good at saying 'no comment,' since before the grand jury, so I took it."[275] He would also do color commentary on the ACC TV Game of the Week during the basketball season. It was a situation he would have to live with.[276]

On 2 November 1986, the *Washington Post* carried a story by Novak, by that time a recognized fan and good friend of the ousted coach. It was headlined "'Lefty,' They Done You Wrong" and in its fourth paragraph, the scapegoat label was *"officially"* applied. Honesty compelled Novak to admit Driesell had been both target and victim of the "mutual enmity" between himself and area sports writers, and even admitted that a previous incident in 1983, during which "Lefty" had attempted to influence events and public opinion surrounding one of his players (the previously mentioned Herman Veal), had only made things worse and probably helped convict him in Slaughter's eyes long before the Bias tragedy occurred three years later. He also called the quick hiring of Wade "either insensitive" or the "final insult." Speaking for many, the article closed with: "How many of us treasured the Driesell years at College Park and how we deplore the way he has been treated."[277]

Two years later, another lengthy article in Washington, D.C.'s now defunct *Regardie's* magazine seemed to seek absolution for Slaughter, who would soon thereafter exit Maryland and the mess he had made for the presidency of tiny Occidental College on the other side of the country (Los Angeles), about as far removed and as he could get. It was entitled "The Education of John Slaughter" and attempted to recant and recast the sad string of events that had transformed a "personal tragedy" into an "institutional crisis." Its most telling statement involved the chancellor's personal assessment of the basketball program, which differed completely from boosters like Novak. While justifiably proud of the fact Driesell had developed a winner without the NCAA violations that had plagued so many other successful, Division I programs, "Slaughter believed this clean record to be a façade that concealed a much more significant fact, (namely that) many student athletes were graduating from his university without the educational skills they needed."

Whether true or not, there's little doubt his ensuing crusade to redeem Terrapin Athletics was an abysmal failure and displayed an essential lack of judgment so necessary to big-time college athletics and administration. Lack of trust within the athletic department and Wade's NCAA violations set Maryland basketball back by years. Although not alone when it came to fault in the aftermath of the Bias tragedy, it's now fairly obvious that the outgoing chancellor's choices only made things worse, leaving it to others to pick up the pieces (some would say it took two decades) once he was gone.[278]

Needless to say, "Lefty" Driesell was not among them. But while awards originally scheduled for Slaughter were canceled in the wake of the controversy, Driesell continued to be appreciated—by the Maryland House of Delegates and the Senate, where he "was vigorously applauded" while being honored with resolutions from both houses, and by the Maryland fraternities and sororities, who made him the only person to ever receive such a tribute from the university's entire Greek system.[279]

14

From Coaching Purgatory to the Shenandoah

Bobby Ross and "Lefty" Driesell became good friends during their time together at the University of Maryland. They still are. In fact, Driesell wasn't the only high-profile coach to leave College Park as a result of the Bias tragedy. Although he wasn't forced out, Ross was also a victim of administration mandates, causing him to leave for the greener pastures of Georgia Tech in football-rich Atlanta rather than accept new admission standards likely to put his Maryland gridiron program at almost certain disadvantages. Remarkably, his decision to leave came on the way home from a 42–10 win at the University of Virginia in the 1986 regular season finale, but also at the end of the worst of his five Terrapin football seasons, a 5–5–1 campaign that had been plagued from the start by distractions resulting from the Bias controversy.[280]

Also overwhelmed by the situation after only five years on the job (having replaced his mentor, Kehoe), Maryland Athletic Director Dick Dull had resigned nearly a month before Driesell and with both of his colleagues gone, Ross wanted no part of the coming, self-imposed scrutiny Slaughter and his administration cronies were about to implement. By 1 December 1986, Ross had resigned. *Born Ready* stated he told his players he was leaving because "at that time, they needed a change" and he needed a change. "The media talked a lot about poor facilities being a big deal," he reportedly said. "I would have liked better facilities, but that wasn't the reason. There was no athletic director who was going to give me better answers. Not having a defined direction and (with) all the other distractions, I felt it was time to move on." In 1990, Ross would lead Georgia Tech to a share of the college football national championship. From there he would go on to lead two NFL teams, including one to a Super Bowl.[281]

Meanwhile, Driesell would spend two years in coaching purgatory. Just before the start of the 1986–1987 season, Jefferson-Raycom offered him the chance to provide TV commentary for weekly ACC games and this brief interlude on the tube would prove a nice way of staying involved without over-commitment.[282] An ACC Tournament preview by Jim Schlosser of the *Greensboro News-Record* in 1987 revealed his enjoyment and relaxation at that moment. "If I don't coach, this is what I want to do—I like the ACC," the story quoted him as saying. "I know all the conference coaches and schools, and have no desire to do any other games. I've done my travelling."[283]

After all, with his status as a tenured professor and his new Maryland boss, replacement AD Lew Perkins, telling him to "just come to work and do what you want," it was easy for Driesell to transition to the once-a-week telecasts with veteran play-by-play announcer Mike Patrick. "Let's face it, I didn't have to do a lot of homework," he reminded. "It seemed hard at first with someone giving me instructions in my ear while I'm trying to talk, but with practice I got used to it and got to be pretty good."[284]

But despite the knowledge, down-home style, and easy-to-understand insight he brought to ACC telecasts, TV was not in "Lefty" Driesell's long-range plans. Instead, his future was about to return to the sidelines with a Colonial Athletic Association school in his home state.

Harrisonburg, Virginia, at the center of the beautiful Shenandoah Valley, had become well known in college basketball circles in those days as the birthplace of ACC giant Ralph Sampson. It's also home to James Madison University. Originally founded as a women's college in 1908, JMU didn't admit its first male students until 1946, but by the time the Dukes (team name in honor of second college president, Samuel Page Duke) came calling on Driesell in 1988, they had already been to three straight NCAA Division I Tournaments under former coach Lou Campanelli in the early 1980s, and recorded some impressive first round tournament wins over Georgetown, Ohio State, and West Virginia.[285]

After Campanelli left JMU for the brighter Pac-10 Conference lights at the University of California (where he led four other teams to the NCAA Tournament before being fired with 10 games left in the 1993 season over profanity laced tirades), his assistant and handpicked successor, John Thurston, stayed less than three years at JMU before opting for a less pressurized athletic director/head coaching role at Division II Wingate University. His departure followed a 6–11 start in 1987–1988 and despite the fact he had been CAA Coach of the Year the previous season when the team was 20–10. Interim coach Tom McCorry directed the final 11 games that year, going 4–7 the rest of the way.[286]

The previously mentioned Russ Potts, Maryland's former promotional whiz and a longtime Driesell confidant, had by that time become a state senator from northwestern Virginia. This political detour in his otherwise athletics dominated career followed stints as athletic director at Southern Methodist University (SMU) in Dallas and vice president with the Chicago White Sox, as well as the birth of his own sports promotions company out of Winchester, Virginia. His connections with Ed Bridgeforth, a prominent supporter and member of the JMU Board of Visitors for whom the James Madison football stadium is named, led directly to "Lefty's" recruitment for the Dukes head coaching position, something Potts has since had second thoughts about.[287]

"In retrospect, I'm not so sure either of us did the right thing by him going to JMU. Because of the limitations of that league (CAA's normal status as a one-bid conference to the NCAA Tournament), it might have been better for him to sit out a year or so longer," Potts explained.

> I don't think there's any question that if he had still been available, some other school from one of the power conferences, for instance the SEC (Southeastern Conference), would have eventually come calling once the Bias thing settled down. With his southern charm, he would have fit in perfectly at a place like Auburn, Georgia, or Alabama—any school in the South or Southwest that had a strong president. In fact, if I had known how Maryland would turn out, I can promise you I would have tried to bring him to SMU. He would have been unbelievable in a place like Dallas. With all the money that school had at the time, the sky would have been the limit for basketball with him running the show.

One such example of a *"big-time winner"* resurfacing in a power conference following dismissal from a major university in another would come a few years later with Bobby Knight's fiery exit from the University of Indiana over repeated anger management and player mistreatment issues. Knight was hired to coach Texas Tech just one year later. Other examples would include Jim Harrick being hired by the state universities of both Rhode Island and Georgia after dismissal from UCLA for lying about falsified recruiting receipts, and Eddie Sutton resurfacing at Oklahoma State following numerous recruiting violations under his watch at Kentucky, so as Potts speculated, with a little more time (and perhaps, patience), the prospects of a Driesell return to the big-time would have probably come back from the Bias abyss.[288]

Nevertheless, once "Lefty" consented to the JMU job, he would remain there for nine years despite other Division I inquiries, according to Potts, who was at the news conference in Harrisonburg the day he was introduced. "The ironic thing with 'Lefty' is that he's never had so much as a jaywalking violation before or since. At Maryland he was the fall guy, the guy in the wrong place at the wrong time. It was a grave injustice to him and his career," he added.[289]

The radio play-by-play voice of the Dukes for all nine years of Driesell's JMU tenure, Jim Britt, remembered well the speculation and excitement generated by his coming. "I can even remember the first reported sighting," Britt said.

> Somebody saw him in Harrisonburg with the job open and before you knew it, the Washington (DC) TV network affiliates were all speculating that he was taking the job. I will never forget the day he was introduced at the (JMU) Convocation Center. I don't know how many hundreds were there, but everything those first couple of years was huge. The bar was raised in recruiting, scheduling, everything. He was like a rock star. The first game he ever coached at JMU was in Hawaii and you know "Lefty's" fondness for the beach, so we decided to tape the pregame coach's show on the beach at Waikiki. Almost immediately, there are all these people there who recognized him, wishing him well, asking for his autograph. It was like that everywhere we went.[290]

Steve Hood, one of his last Maryland recruits, would follow him to James Madison as a transfer after two years as a Terrapin and become a two-time CAA Player of the Year and second-round NBA Draft choice. A tall and talented shooting guard, Hood had averaged 10.8 points per game his first two years at Maryland, but would ratchet that up to more than 20 points per outing his final two years at JMU. His name still dots the Dukes' record book, including points in a season (682 in 1989–1990), three-point percentage (48.2 percent that same year), free throws attempted (215 in 1990–1991), and three-point percentage for a career (46.4 percent). In 2005, Hood was inducted into the JMU Sports Hall of Fame along with his coach.[291]

Britt fondly recalled some of the high points of those JMU years, including ESPN's first midnight telecast of a CAA game, a blowout win over fellow conference contender Richmond in front of a raucous, packed house in Harrisonburg. Then there was the 77–76 CAA Tournament Championship win over Old Dominion in 1993–1994 when JMU came from 19 points down and "Lefty" ran his "swinging gate," a play designed to get his best shooter, Kent Culuko, the last-second, game-winning shot from the corner. "After the play was called, he confided to me later that he couldn't bear to watch," Britt said. "But that was just one example of how he consistently put those teams in position to win championships."[292]

With respected coaches like the University of Richmond's Dick Tarrant, the Colonial was already a good, close-knit league and with "Lefty" at the helm, JMU would win the conference regular season championship five straight times. Four times the Dukes would play in the NIT following a string of CAA Tournament heartbreaks before finally breaking through for the elusive NCAA bid in 1993–1994. From the 10–18 remains he inherited, Driesell's first seven JMU teams would go 16–14, 20–11, 19–10, 21–11, 21–9, 20–10, and 16–13 despite always playing a tough schedule that included non-conference matchups with as many teams from the six power conferences as possible.[293] "I always wanted to play the best teams and we beat the likes of Purdue, Florida, Auburn, and BYU while I was at James Madison," he proudly remembered. "We only had the one bad year with over 20 losses when I just flat overscheduled."[294]

Included on his non-conference schedule that year were the likes of Illinois State, Auburn, Butler, and Houston. Only one of those was a win and the Dukes finished 10–20 and just 6–10 in the CAA. The next year they improved to 16–13 and 8–8, but that wasn't enough to keep then JMU president Ronald Carrier, the same guy who hired "Lefty" and emphasized athletics, from moving to replace his 65-year-old head coach once Driesell mentioned retirement. That apparently happened during a postseason interview the day after JMU lost to Old Dominion in overtime, 62–58, in the 1996–1997 CAA Tournament Finals. According to an article by Mike Hodge in the *Harrisonburg Daily News Record*, that's when "Lefty" stated, "Next year will be my last. This is a time-consuming job. There's a lot of pressure. I've done it for nearly 40 years. It's time to do something else in my life."[295]

His comment was made with his contract coming to an end, but apparently took administration officials by surprise. The same newspaper article indicated "Lefty's" contract was set to expire that spring, but Carrier had promised Driesell the previous fall that he could stay at Madison until he got his 700th win. It added that he intended to retire even if he didn't get the 17 wins necessary to reach 700. "Next year I want to win and if we can go to the NCAAs, I think we'll have a pretty good shot," he said at the time. "I don't know what I'll do. That's why I hesitated in saying anything."[296]

Just a few days later, another Mike Hodge article confirmed that Chuck Driesell, by then a JMU assistant for nine years, hoped to succeed his father. It said, "Chuck Driesell is one of a handful of obvious candidates" and quoted the younger Driesell as saying, "No question. I love JMU. I love the school. I love the program. We have a good nucleus of talent returning and with the kids we have coming (two recruiting commitments at the time). At the same time, some things you can't control. Hopefully the people making the decision feel the same way I do." That story also indicated "Lefty" had already lobbied Carrier for Chuck to succeed him. He said he felt Chuck should get the job because "he has helped make the program consistently competitive in the CAA," adding, "I hope Chuck gets the job. He's worked his butt off." A JMU player at the time, Ned Felton, was also quoted as hoping the younger Driesell got the job. He said, "He knows what the players can and can't do for us on the court. All the players love coach C. He's young, but he's not that young. He understands us."[297]

Driesell has since confirmed that he indeed hoped to sign an extension that he could later hand off to Chuck in hopes of ensuring him time to rebuild the program and establish himself as a Division I head coach. Deep down "Lefty" felt at least two seasons would be necessary before it could come all the way back to the 20-win level.[298] Carrier, however, wasn't interested. In fact, another *Daily News Record* follow-up in 2006 listed 5 March 1997 as the date that "changed" the JMU program. Apparently, that was the day Driesell got a call from then JMU Athletic Director Don Lemish while en route to his beach house letting him know his contract would not be renewed, "effectively firing the man that had led the Dukes to four 20-win seasons in nine years."[299] According to Potts, Carrier has since confided to him that his angry reaction to "Lefty's" pronouncements at the time was among his biggest mistakes.[300] When asked for comment, however, Carrier provided no reply.[301]

Meanwhile Driesell's assessment of the Dukes' immediate future would be proven accurate when his eventual replacement, Sherman Dillard, finished only 11–16 the next season and enjoyed just two winning years out of seven (and no conference championships) between 1997–1998 and 2003–2004.[302] By that time, "Lefty" had retired with more than 100 wins at yet another Division I school. To his disappointment, he had done it without Chuck, who he hoped to bring with him to Georgia State University before encountering a Georgia nepotism statute that prohibited hiring or supervising one's immediate family at any of the state's public institutions of higher learning[303] (something that obviously didn't seem to matter two years later at the University of Georgia when Harrick hired his son, Jim Harrick, Jr., as one of his assistant coaches, a questionable situation that would prove especially so in 2003 when both were fired for academic and NCAA-related improprieties).[304]

Driesell's final overall record at JMU was 159–111 and he was CAA Coach of the Year in both 1989–1990 and 1991–1992. While there, with his four kids grown and on their own, he and Joyce built a home with a beautiful Shenandoah view aiming towards retirement.[305] But retirement was not to be when Georgia State University came calling with one last coaching assignment—perhaps his toughest assignment ever.

15

One More Time for the Program Builder

Dave Cohen has been the radio voice of Georgia State University Basketball for over 30 years. With play-by-play aspirations while still a student working for the campus radio station, he felt extremely lucky when he was offered the Panthers' broadcast job at age 21 in 1983. He confirmed as much when he said, "I felt really fortunate to be in that position at such a young age. To do play-by-play for a Division I program with all the travel and people I met was exciting. It was an eye-opening experience and I loved every minute."[306]

Such enthusiasm during his early years with the Panthers was commendable, especially given the team's lack of success in the Sun Belt Conference. In fact, Georgia State was considered the *"losingest"* Division I men's basketball program in the nation during the late 1970s and 1980s, when records like 5–21, 7–20, 4–23, and even 2–26 were commonplace, and 14–14 was a good year, the team's first non-losing season, in 1988–1989.[307]

Playing in a third floor gymnasium in downtown Atlanta, the concrete commuter campus was a tough sell when it came to recruiting the kind of players necessary to compete at the Division I level. Attendance was (and is) another constant problem given the exodus of people leaving the city for Atlanta's far-flung residential suburbs every weekday, including students and staff, and the fact allegiances always trended towards more established major college programs and the professional teams that dominate the Atlanta sports scene. Weekends were hardly better, as Sun Belt schedules (and later those of the Trans America Athletic and Atlantic Sun Conferences) rarely offered the kind of opposition that would draw people back to downtown from surrounding distances far exceeding the normal drive times of most college towns. "Because I was young, I guess the losing didn't bother me so much," Cohen recently recalled. "I tried to keep it all in perspective and just do my job."[308]

Such acceptance of defeat, however, seemed to be changing when a local high school coaching legend, Bob Reinhart, was hired to lead the Panthers to what most believed would finally be an era of success in 1985. Joining him were a group of major college transfers from throughout the area, mostly products of Metro Atlanta high schools who, for one reason or another, were not happy with their status at universities like Georgia, Florida, Clemson, and Auburn. Multitalented, they all sat out a year for what figured to be their chance to dominate a weak league under Reinhart's respected guidance. Unfortunately, it didn't work out that way, as lack of chemistry and better-than-advertised mid-major opposition combined to slow much-anticipated progress, and it wasn't until 1990–1991 that Reinhart finally got over the hump with a veteran team of more traditional recruits.[309] Despite finishing only 16–15, that team surprised everyone by winning the TAAC Tournament and advancing to the NCAA Tournament.

That team also garnered Reinhart three more years at the helm, only one of which produced a winning record. Meanwhile, his top assistant, Carter Wilson, somehow followed as head coach before he too was let go following a 31–50 overall record over three additional years. That amazing display of administration patience finally came to an end following the 1996–1997 season (about a week before "Lefty" Driesell parted ways with JMU—see prologue).[310] Amid all the mediocrity,

Cohen will never forget being down by 50 points (that's right, 50) in a game at Clemson during Reinhart's fifth season. "That's the one time I let my frustrations get the better of me and said something I shouldn't have on air," he remembered.[311]

But Cohen wasn't the only one growing frustrated at Georgia State. The way "Lefty" remembered it, after confirming interest; it wasn't long before Panther Athletic Director Orby Moss called for an interview. "My daughter was living in the Atlanta area and really wanted me to consider the job," he said.

> It was like "please, please"—she really talked me into coming. So when Orby and Dr. (Carl) Patton (GSU president) offered the job, I already had my mind made up. I still wanted to coach. That state rule (nepotism) that kept me from hiring Chuck was something I wasn't happy about, but at least I was able to bring my other assistant from James Madison, Phil Cunningham. The office situation was awful, but hey, it was Atlanta, the greatest city in the South.

According to Driesell, James Madison's facilities were much better than Georgia State. "At JMU I was able to use the campus and dorm life as a positive, but at Georgia State I sure couldn't sell facilities, so I decided I would use the good academics and playing in Atlanta in my recruiting sales pitch. I also depended on jucos (junior college transfers) and four-year transfers a lot more than ever before," he's stated.[312]

From the very beginning, Driesell's approach to building a program was far different from his predecessors. "He was like a carnival barker, always selling and promoting," Cohen said.

> Things like the money-back guarantee, where season ticket holders would get a refund for every home game the Panthers lost—that was his idea and it got national attention. He was like a cross between a coach and an itinerant preacher. That's what made him so valuable to a school like

Georgia State. Without someone like "Lefty," a school like Georgia State gets lost among all the pro and college teams. No other coach had ever forced Georgia State Athletics to grow up like he did. "Lefty" was the first person to put a face on Georgia State Athletics. People took notice. It was a monumental hire. As much as Reinhart generated interest locally, "Lefty" generated interest nationally. Even after recruiting Bill Curry to start football, "Lefty" is still the best hire in the history of Georgia State Athletics.[313]

In fact, "Lefty" was always trying to figure out ways to put Georgia State on even more of the map. On more than one occasion he suggested better known color commentators to Cohen as alternatives to the ones the school could afford. "Truth be known, he would have brought in Bob Costas and let me go if he could have," Cohen laughed in remembrance. "He wanted the program to be big-time and he was always coming up with some off-the-wall idea to help make it happen."[314]

In his first season at the Georgia State helm, 1997–1998, with a team whose tallest starter was only 6 feet, 6 inches, and whose star was a diminutive, holdover point guard (Rodney Hamilton), Driesell's Panthers immediately jumped from five straight losing years to 16–12 and 11–5 in the Atlantic Sun Conference. It was the first of five straight winning seasons under The Old Lefthander. Along the way was a 1998–1999 season opener against perennial Big East Conference power Georgetown in the Georgia Dome, an event that drew almost 10,000 and would have never been possible before "Lefty." Just one game later, he recorded his milestone 700th career win. The next year, Tarkanian also brought his Fresno State quintet to Atlanta for a much-publicized game at the GSU Sports Arena. And there were plenty of significant wins, including a 91–79 victory at the University of Georgia to open 2000–2001, a portent of what was to come the remainder of that historic season in Atlanta.[315] "I had a pretty good feeling that team was going to be good and it became reality in the season opener at UGA when we ran the Bulldogs out of their own building," Cohen fondly remembered.[316]

After back-to-back 17-win seasons in 1998–1999 and 1999–2000, Driesell had finally stockpiled all the talent he would need to dominate the Trans America. Attracting some major college transfers, who wanted to stay and/or return to the Atlanta area, and some game-changing juco stars from throughout the Southeast, "Lefty" coached his way to 29 wins, his most ever, in his 39th year as a Division I head coach at age 70.[317]

Among his standouts were guards Kevin Morris, a much ballyhooed Georgia Tech signee who started for the Yellow Jackets before starring for the Panthers, and Shenard Long, the TransAmerica Player of the Year after starring at nearby Tucker High School, transferring from Georgetown University, and then leading four starters in double figures with 18 points per game as a senior. In addition, 6-foot, 4-inch defensive ace Darryl Cooper proved invaluable in limiting the other team's top scorer and contributing his own dozen or so points per contest, and 6-foot, 7-inch Thomas Terrell, a junior college standout, achieved stardom almost immediately, averaging 16.4 points and 7.5 rebounds his first year and 20.5 and 7.3 his second.[318] "We finished 29–5, but could have very easily been 31–3," Cohen recalled. "We lost a couple of league games on the road when Stetson and Troy State shot over 60 percent from the field and could have beaten just about anybody in the country on those particular nights."[319] Those Panthers won their other 17 conference games by an average of 15 points per contest and their only other losses were at nationally ranked, non-conference toughies Creighton and the University of New Mexico.[320]

After rolling to the TAAC Tournament Finals where they easily dispatched Troy State, 79–55, they earned an NCAA bid against a Big 10 Conference power, the University of Wisconsin, which had made it all the way to the Final Four just a year earlier.[321] "Obviously, I felt really good about our team and the best season in school history, but I was unsure about how we would match up against a Big 10, Final Four team from the year before," Cohen admitted.[322]

Meanwhile, "Lefty's" theme as the season progressed had become "This ain't no Mickey Mouse team," a reference he coined during a road trip to Orlando, Florida, when the Panthers posed for a group photo at Disney World.[323] "Even somebody referring to us as a mid-major rubbed him the wrong way," Cohen remembered.

> That team just had great chemistry with him coaching and all those stars coming together with an all-for-one attitude. It really put him back in the national spotlight and there was a lot of hype when we were sent to the same NCAA Regional as the University of Maryland (with first and second rounds at Boise, Idaho). The way we were playing, I think he had to feel pretty good about being in a position to play his old team.[324]

And that matchup with the Terrapins became reality when the Panthers recovered from a halftime deficit to overtake Wisconsin in the first round on a last minute, four-point play by Cooper. It included a three-point basket ("the biggest shot in GSU basketball history," according to Cohen) and resulting free throw when he was also fouled. That was followed by Long's driving layup just seconds later "that barely avoided being blocked," providing the winning margin in the Panthers'

50–49 upset victory, their first ever in NCAA Tournament play.[325] Two nights later, however, Maryland prevailed over Driesell's Panthers in the second round, 79–60, with most of the same players who would go on to win the Terrapins' first national title in Atlanta just a year later, 2001–2002.[326]

Ironically, that would also be Driesell's last full season in Atlanta. After producing his second straight 20-win team at Georgia State (20–11), his Panthers lost by one point to Florida Atlantic in the Atlantic Sun Finals, 76–75, before also losing in the first round of the NIT, 64–62, at Tennessee Tech. The next year, 2002–2003, they were off to a 4–6 start when their 72-year-old head coach suddenly decided to take off his sneakers and step down at mid-season. [327] Plagued by illness, residual discomfort from neck surgery a few years earlier, travel fatigue, and a sudden lack of desire, Driesell's decision didn't surprise program insiders, many of whom had expected him to step down the year before if Georgia State had managed a second straight conference championship. It also paved the way for GSU Assistant Coach Michael Perry to inherit the interim opportunity that ultimately led to him coaching the Panthers for five more years. "Speaking selfishly for myself and the program, I would have liked for him ('Lefty') to stay long enough to get 800 wins, but it wasn't a shock," Cohen stated. "I just think he was worn down health-wise by the day-to-day rigors of college coaching and suddenly, 786 wins was enough."[328]

Perry fondly recalled his years with "Lefty" and his transition to head coach when Driesell retired. He said,

> His energy and enthusiasm even in the twilight of his career was unbelievable. I can't imagine how energized he must have been when he was younger. John Lucas told me once that he thought the big city of Atlanta actually rejuvenated

him. He created an atmosphere where every day was interesting and one where we (coaching staff) were all involved in everything. He really taught you how to run a program. There's always been a connection and kinship among all the coaches who worked under The Lefthander because we all learned and experienced so many of the same things. He was demanding and held you accountable, but he treated you like family.

Speaking specifically about Driesell's recruiting prowess, Perry said:

He was the best ever at going into the home and never blinked an eye when going up against major schools for the best players in the country. In fact, with The Lefthander you almost had to have two lists, one with the top recruits in the country that he still wanted to go after and one with the players you had a realistic chance of signing at Georgia State. At the same time, it was amazing how many of the top recruits we were in on and the approach he could come up with on a visit. The bigger the recruit the more fired up he was. He knew that if he just went in there and it was apples to apples he couldn't win, so he would hit the floor running about how their "stock was gonna drop if they went to one of the big schools and played only 15 or 20 minutes a game, whereas they could come with us and average 25 or 30 points a game." He could be totally consumed in the moment; moments I will never forget.

About "Lefty's" coaching style, Perry added:

Another time he was especially fired up was right before the Maryland game in the NCAA. You could tell how much it meant to him. He had even told our players before they beat Wisconsin, you get this one for me and I'll get the next one for you. Like a lot of teams, Maryland used a 1–3–1 trap when you were taking the ball out in your end and most teams just throw over the top to avoid the trap, but "Lefty" never wanted to accept that you couldn't find a way to attack that defense. It was an example of how he always wanted to find ways to counter the other team's strengths. Even with only one day to prepare, I can remember spending time in practice before that game with him addressing that issue. He did not want to give in to just inbounding over the top. I worked with Dick Tarrant and some other good coaches, but nobody was better prepared than The Lefthander. There were lots of times he wouldn't give in to conventional wisdom…he was always looking for something better. He took the Maryland loss hard because he knew we could have finished that game so much better. We had some players who disappeared in the tournament. Maybe it was their (Maryland's) size and strength finally getting to us, but he took it hard and let the players know he was disappointed with their effort.

As for Driesell's abrupt departure, Perry recalled:

Kelvin Sampson (former Oklahoma and Indiana coach) told me once that lifetime coaches like "Lefty" never retire in an orderly fashion—that he would probably decide spur of the moment just to walk away and that's exactly what happened. When he decided it was time, he told me the job would be mine and it was an easy transition because I had recruited all our players and established a level of trust with them, as well as the fact he had given me so much responsibility already. The administration went along and the next year, my first full season as head coach (2003–2004), we equaled the second most wins in school history at 20–9.[329]

In fall 2001, Perry also went through one of the toughest experiences a coach could ever have to deal with alongside Driesell. That's when Georgia State center Andre Tooks, a 6-foot, 10-inch junior college transfer from Shawnee-Mission, Kansas, was seriously injured in an auto accident in downtown Atlanta. The Toyota truck Tooks was driving was hit by another vehicle whose driver had run a red light. At first it seemed he might rally and regain consciousness, but with his mother en route by plane he died at nearby Grady Hospital from injuries sustained in the crash.[330]

There's a very tall escalator at Atlanta's Hartsfield-Jackson Airport that's very familiar to frequent travelers as they re-enter the terminal for baggage claim and ground transportation. That's where Driesell and Perry were waiting for Tooks's mother as she made her way as quickly as she could to try and be at her son's side. Surprised by them being at the airport when she got there, their reasons were revealed soon enough with grief counselors stationed in the airport chapel nearby. "It's one of the toughest things I've ever been a part of," Perry confirmed.

> Coach (Driesell) had to tell her Andre had passed and that was extremely tough on him. Afterwards you could see it brought back to the surface the other players lost on his watch, Bias, Owen Brown, and Chris Patton (all three at Maryland). I guess you're never prepared for something like that, but his love and compassion for all his players and their families really showed through at that moment. We were all devastated, but he knew he needed to be strong for everyone else. He had been through it several times before, but you could see it took a real toll on him personally and physically.[331]

Even in retirement, he would continue to watch his former assistant coaches become head coaches in the Division I ranks. Along with Perry, Cunningham would ultimately get a Division I head job at Troy University (formerly Troy State) in 2013,[332] and Travis Williams, a former Georgia State player before "Lefty" became coach and the last full-time addition to his final Panther staff, would go on to a promising 18–15 record in his first year as the head coach at Tennessee State in 2012–2013. Both marked continuations of the "Lefty" coaching tree;

of success stories like Holland and Raveling, Harrington and Purnell, and the previously unmentioned Gale Catlett, who won 565 games alone between 1972 and 2002 at the University of Cincinnati and West Virginia following an early career stint with Driesell at Davidson.[333] Like the others, Williams would offer immediate testimony to the advantages of working under The Lefthander when at the end of his first campaign he remarked, "Getting to watch him ('Lefty') coach up close and personal. Being able to watch him and see his success—that was a great influence on me."[334]

16

Renounced, but Finally Honored

On 25 January 2012, Nicole Auerbach reported in *USA Today* what the *Baltimore Sun* had already made public— "Lefty" Driesell was not happy about the University of Maryland's decision to name its basketball court at the Comcast Center in honor of retiring men's basketball coach Gary Williams. The quote from Driesell read: "It's not fair to my players that they put Gary Williams name on the court. It's a disservice to players such as Tom McMillen, John Lucas, Len Elmore, Brad Davis, Greg Manning, Adrian Branch, and Steve Sheppard."[335]

Thus were documented feelings that probably shouldn't have been aired. *"Sour grapes"* was undoubtedly the reaction of many readers when they first learned that the coach who put Maryland basketball on the map (before being forced out) was not happy about the new Terrapin court being named in honor of the coach who led them to their only national title in 2002. Finally surpassed in wins at the school after Williams coached there for 21 years, four more than his 17, Driesell nevertheless had reason to feel *"slighted,"* especially where his players were concerned. Whether or not that was reason enough to make his feelings known remains debatable, but once again, "Lefty" being "Lefty," it was understandable that he would.

After all, wasn't it enough that the bad taste of Maryland's dismissal still lingered, 26 years later? Now, adding insult to injury, the school honored one and in doing so renounced the other. Sure Williams had the national title (although at least one veteran UM hoops observer, Russ Potts, claims there's no way his 2002 team would have ever beaten Driesell's better Terrapin quintets), but with such equal success, was elevating one over the other really an appropriate thing to do.

While many basketball powers have their obvious patron saints, John Wooden at UCLA, Rupp at Kentucky, Krzyzewski at Duke, there were two extraordinary winners at Maryland and choosing one over the other for such a singular honor in modern basketball circles had to hurt, especially at 80 years of age. Sure, Driesell's name had generously been applied to the court at Georgia State after his five years there, but that was more acknowledgement of rescue and resuscitation of a previously moribund program than prolonged greatness. He was certainly honored and appreciative, but that was for the back end of his career, not the zenith, and certainly not in the much brighter lights of the ACC.

Perhaps his name on the court at Georgia State's third floor gym could actually serve as a metaphor for his entire career—honored and appreciated, but not glorified—at least not the way many of his coaching contemporaries had been. Perhaps that's also why Maryland did see fit to finally honor him with a life-size bas relief likeness of himself at the Comcast Center in April 2013. But wasn't that more a way of making up for past wrongs, both distant and recent, than pure celebration? Would "Lefty's" likeness have ever adorned the Comcast Center if not for Gary's name on the court? Regrettably, probably not.[336]

One had only to go back a decade earlier, when Cole Field House, the big old house that "Lefty" filled and made famous, was closed in favor of the new Comcast Center (deemed "the house that Gary built") to find another perceived slight. That's when Bob Cohn and David Elfin documented in the *Washington Times* that Driesell had been "conspicuous by his absence" at the final game in Cole and, in fact, had not even been invited.[337]

Admittedly still coaching his own team at the time, Georgia State, Driesell played down the non-invite by stating, "It doesn't make any difference to me. My feelings weren't hurt. It would have been nice to see all my players, but I got to see them on TV." Nevertheless, others were justifiably upset. Potts, by then a Virginia state senator, remarked, "I thought it was in poor taste and I'm extremely disappointed. You can't obliterate history. When you think of Cole, you think of 'Lefty' and his magnetism and energy that took that program from among the nation's worst to a national power."[338]

Potts and Harrington were also critical of the decision not to invite Kehoe, who was credited in the *Baltimore Sun* with the comment: "I'm disappointed that I wasn't asked to come, but it's absolutely wrong that 'Lefty' Driesell, the man who started it all, was not invited. It's sinful. I was shocked when he told me he wasn't invited."[339]

Among those who were on hand was Millikan, the coach when Cole opened, and many of the great players from Maryland's past, including McMillen, who stated, "I thought about it when he wasn't there. He was very much a part of Cole and it would have been nice to see him honored. That's all I need to say, really." Ten years later, after the court honor also went to Williams, it would be McMillen who would finally make his feelings known, leading the chorus in the development and dedication of "Lefty's" bas relief sculpture. Appropriately, its location in the Comcast Center is next to a preserved section of the Cole Field House court.[340]

A remarkable and somewhat ironic tribute was also given to Driesell at the bas relief's unveiling by current University of Maryland Chancellor William Kirwan, who authored a letter (to "friends and colleagues") that stated, "From my perspective, 'Lefty's' greatest contributions are found in the impact he had on the lives of his student athletes. 'Lefty' had a genuine focus on his players and pushed them for success on and off the court. 'Lefty's' players always had one of the highest graduation rates in Division I."[341] Needless to say, perceptions had changed a lot in 27 years in the UM chancellor's office.

Termed "perhaps the best coach who never made the Final Four and without a doubt one of the most colorful and entertaining coaches to (ever) walk a sideline" by Ron Green, Sr., of the *Charlotte Observer* when he retired from Georgia State in 2003, Driesell relocated close to his Norfolk roots once retirement was official.[342] It was Joyce's love of the sea and beach, however, that led them to ultimately settle in a fourth-floor condo with ocean views throughout at nearby Virginia Beach. Good restaurants, especially seafood, and everything else they need are within easy driving (or even walking) distance and their home is as open and inviting as the couple themselves. An office adorned floor to ceiling with the same photographs, plaques, and framed memorabilia that was an ever-expanding part of Driesell's coaching career, wherever he was, now occupies a central location off the main hallway. There's also a storage room filled with filing cabinets, each one chocked full of other remnants of a legendary career spanning nearly five decades of success.[343]

Still a local icon, with celebratory clippings and past accomplishments to be found in establishments throughout the Tidewater region, Driesell is like a favorite son returned from the competitive wars of yesteryear as he moves through the community, acknowledging old friends and well-wishers, usually in his trademark warm-up suits, apparently standard attire for basketball coaches no matter what their age. While relegated to walking with a cane and by somewhat limited mobility, especially when fatigue or the aches and pains of past surgeries set in, Driesell continues to live via the college game he helped shape and has always loved. With Chuck now a head coach at The Citadel in the same Southern Conference where "Lefty" got his start, strategy, recruiting, and suggestions are never far from Driesell's mind. He readily admits to watching as many games on television (or even via computer) during the collegiate season as possible. When the season ends, he often struggles for something to do.[344]

A lifelong Washington Redskins fan, a loyalty solidified by his years and associations while living in the Washington area, he has particular affinity for Robert Griffin III and the extensive rehab that was expected of the sensational young quarterback following his star-studded (but injury riddled) first NFL season, and he wasn't at all surprised when Redskins Coach Mike Shanahan had to be fired following the team's total meltdown in 2013. "With the way 'RG3' plays, I will always worry about him staying healthy," Driesell freely admitted.

While glad to be off the road and away from the travel requirements faced all those years, he still makes his way to area games and events, especially when his revered presence is requested, as well as the Final Four and its annual coaches' conference. He also maintains several personal and/or family related rental properties, including the house where he grew up and his beach house, about three hours away in Delaware. In fact, like *homeowners* all along the Atlantic Seaboard, hurricanes remain a concern, one he's been lucky to dodge so far but one that still requires awareness and his occasional attention.[345]

His family—grown, expanded, and moved on—remains a source of pride. A November 2010 article in the *Atlanta Journal/Constitution* spoke to such things when it detailed Pam's ascension to the senior pastorate role (atop a ministerial staff of five) at prestigious Trinity Presbyterian Church in Atlanta's affluent Buckhead section and Chuck's acceptance of the previously mentioned Citadel head coaching job, positions they both still held at this writing, as well as all they had learned from their famous father. Pam has two boys and Chuck two boys and a girl. Meanwhile, his other daughters, Patti and Carolyn, reside with their families in Atlanta and West Chester, Pennsylvania, respectively, the first a nutritionist and the latter a contented housewife, and both mothers of three. Among his brood are two grandsons just beginning coaching careers after playing throughout high school and college, and like proud grandfathers everywhere, "Lefty" has tried, through the years, to see as many of their games as possible. After all, it's the one thing he never gets tired of—basketball.[346]

While some honors eluded Driesell, others of a more unique nature did not. For instance, when *Sports Illustrated* came out at the end of the 20th century with its "50 from 50," the 50 greatest sports figures from all 50 states, there he was— the only coach of any sport listed among Virginia's all-time greats.[347] Likewise, when *Washingtonian* magazine announced its "45 Who Shaped Washington, 1965–2010," there he was once again, this time sharing space and equal billing with Georgetown's John Thompson and a few more obvious choices, such as Ronald Reagan.[348] There was even the time in 1977 when *Charlotte Magazine* named him (alongside Jimmy Carter) to a list of "outstanding salesmen,"[349] another much-deserved accolade when you think about all those *sales jobs* from his early career. Those kinds of distinctions along with the school, conference, city, and state athletic halls of fame (13 in all) of which he has long been a member ensured his legacy long before larger honors of more recent vintage justifiably came his way. Today, there's even a national basketball award named in his honor—the "Lefty" Driesell Defensive Player of the Year—and a "Lefty" Driesell Defensive All-America Team, both named by CollegiateInsider.com.[350]

While sharing an iconic sports nickname with Baseball Hall of Famer Robert Moses "Lefty" Grove,[351] he also deserves consideration, at least, for the nickname hall of fame along with "Babe," "Bo," and "Magic," other athletic monikers that took on legendary status by actually replacing given names. Now *that's* something Dean never had. Neither did Adolph. While we all recognize basketball sobriquets like "Tark the Shark," "Baron of The Bluegrass," "The Wizard of Westwood," and "Coach K," there's no denying he's the most celebrated hoops coach to achieve nickname immortality to the point of having it recognized as the replacement for his given name. Perhaps the next closest would be current Texas Coach Orlando "Tubby" Smith or the previously mentioned Horace Albert "Bones" McKinney, who was once, so the story goes, connected to "Lefty" in another way...*from beyond the grave.*

It happened at a Wake Forest speaking engagement a year or two after McKinney's death in 1997. Driesell was addressing an attentive assemblage of Demon Deacon boosters when a letter fluttered down from the banquet hall's ceiling. "Somebody in the crowd yelled out 'Must be a message from Bones,' recalled 'Lefty,'" as he fondly remembered the gag. "Turned out they were right," he joked, still going along. "Me and Bones...Guess we were two of a kind."[352]

Genuine to a fault and always a competitor, "Lefty" Driesell remains a living legend of college basketball's growth and development into a national sport and focus. He's a national relic whose 41 Division I head coaching seasons bridged formative years to the modern day—from the earliest stages of the jump shot to most modern players' inability to play with their backs to the basket; from employing his own four corners to one of the earliest, up-and-down, pre-shot clock, three-guard offenses; from a double post offense that always wanted the ball inside to his reluctant acceptance of three-pointers that have changed the game forever; and, perhaps, more than any other coach, from the all-white dominance of Adolph Rupp's Kentucky teams in the South to actually initiating the recruitment and rise of African-American players throughout the region, he's been there, done that. Ultimately defined, like other coaches, by wins and losses, he nevertheless did it with style—his own, for better or worse— and in that sense he's a legend, a legend that may someday finally find his way to Springfield, Massachusetts. Here's hoping it doesn't come too late for him to enjoy.

Epilogue

The Lefthander Speaks Out

Among the most approachable and quotable of Division I head coaches ever, "Lefty" has always been good for an interview or opinion. Now in his 80s, he shared some of those over a five-day period in fall 2012. Some were predictable, some were not. An old-school product, his basic basketball beliefs never changed much through the years, but even he had one or two things he might have done differently and a few notions that might surprise.

On Overworking Players: "At UCLA, John Wooden used to tell his players they should get away from the game in the summer, but now they all play year round. Thinking back, I probably worked my players too hard and that may have been my biggest mistake. Maybe I would have been a better tournament coach. For a while at Davidson I even gave them a day off from practice after a win. They played harder to avoid practice the next day. It was an amazing motivator."

On Taking Players Out Due to Foul Trouble: "I don't agree with automatically taking a guy out when he gets two fouls in the first half or three early in the second, and certainly not four late in the game. Good players learn how to play with fouls. I was talking with my good friend Seth Greenberg while he was at Virginia Tech a couple years ago after they played North Carolina. Tech had a 22-point lead with six minutes left in the first half and Seth took his best inside player out because he had two fouls. The lead shrank from 20 to 10 by halftime and gave Carolina the momentum it needed to come all the way back in the second half. I told Seth, 'Don't do that.' The next game he left him in with two fouls and they beat Maryland going away."

On Basketball Uniforms: "I never liked the short, short pants or some of the longer ones we started seeing a few years ago. The NBA was always the best—somewhere in between. I put names on the back of my players' jerseys my first year at Davidson and I think it's always been a good way for the fans to connect with their team. I've never understood why some people make such a big deal about it not being good for team unity."

On Today's Recruiting Rules: "They're terrible. It hurts the mid-major programs. I would have never been able to accomplish today what I did at Davidson if I couldn't outwork people. I may have been the first NCAA Division I coach to be on call 24 hours a day, 12 months a year. Now the BCS schools have a big advantage...you can't outwork 'em. It's unfair to the mid-majors. Limiting recruiting times favors the big schools or at least the schools with big money. That's too much of an advantage."

On Guarantee Games and Preseason Exhibitions: "I never played guarantee games. The only one I ever agreed to play was at Georgia State when everybody in the conference could bid to host the conference tournament, so I told our athletic director that if he would commit that money ($100,000) to a bid for the conference tournament, I would play one. Before that, home and home is the only way I would play. It's the sporting way to do it. That would help all of basketball by leveling the playing field. Also, preseason exhibition games against Division II and III teams are ridiculous. Regular season games don't mean as much and conference schedules don't mean as much when you don't play every team twice. In other sports, you play preseason exhibitions against teams on your level—pro baseball, pro football, pro basketball, hockey—why not college basketball, especially if you are not going to play that other team twice during the regular season? It would be better competition and you could justifiably charge admission. It would make teams better for the start of the regular season and you could make some extra money. Every team could play two exhibitions, one on the road and one at home."

On the College Shot Clock: "It works. It assures the better team almost always wins. You can't have a slowdown, the way Dean (Smith) used to do it with Phil Ford and his four corners, and the way we did it in our big win over South Carolina my second year at Maryland when they had a much better team."

On His Reputation As a Great Recruiter: "I've never understood it, because I lost out on a lot more good players than I signed. John Feinstein once called me an overrated recruiter and an underrated coach, and he's been covering college basketball a long time. I trust his opinion."

On His Trademark Sideline Stomp During Games: "That's just something I always did with my foot when I got mad, going all the way back to my days as a high school coach. Once when I was at Maryland I stomped on a metal chair on the sidelines at the Greensboro Coliseum and broke it. After the game, a custodian told me I would have to pay for that, so I sent them a check for $25. A few weeks later, they sent the check back because they had auctioned the chair off for charity and made over $500. For years that broken chair was on display at the Ramada Inn in Greensboro, North Carolina. Another time at Davidson, I got mad and broke a door at the Charlotte Coliseum. It fell off its hinges and the facilities manager told me ''Lefty,' you can't come in here slammin' doors and breakin' property.' I just said send me the bill, but the coliseum manager wrote me later and said, "Lefty,' you can break all the doors you want with all the money you are making this place (following several sellouts).'"

On Road Trip Accommodations During His Early Years: "It was called 'local entertainment.' That's how college teams could afford to travel in those days. The home team was responsible for providing housing and food for the visiting team. Most of the time it was somewhere on campus. Dean (Smith—UNC) was the first one whose teams stayed in hotels."

On Being Superstitious: "I wasn't overly superstitious, but I did keep a little mojo (black cat figurine) in my pants pocket at games. At critical moments, I would rub it for luck. Joyce thought it was sacrilegious and didn't want me telling anybody about it, especially our grandchildren."

On the Issue of Paying College Players: "College basketball should always be an amateur sport. College athletes should not be paid unless you want to give them $100 a month or so for laundry money and other incidentals, or whatever is the equivalent of the $15 we got when I was a player. They are still getting free room, food, and the education. If a guy just wants to make money, he can go to Europe and play."

On Transfers and High School Players Going Straight to the NBA: "I don't like the rule about being able to go ahead and transfer (getting closer to home) if they have a sick parent. Allowing that sort of thing can lead to unethical recruiting because coaches are always going to covet the best players. Sitting out a year discourages transfers, but that never stopped me from having some good ones. Also, if a high school player is good enough, they should be allowed to go straight to the NBA. You shouldn't deny anyone the opportunity to make a living. At the same time, college helps the NBA by allowing them to see players against good competition for at least a year.

Two years would be even better for the NBA. Without the one year rule, the NBA is going to make a lot more mistakes."

On College Basketball's Alternating Possession Rule: "I don't like it. There used to be strategy in jump ball situations and they've taken all that out. Besides, it doesn't reward good defense."

On The Three-Point Shot: "That's another thing I've never cared for. There's no inside game anymore, no double posts. Everybody wants to shoot from long range. Players who know how to work for good, medium-range jumpers are few and far between."

On Coaching Camps: "I had the second coaching camp in the South (at Davidson). Campbell University had the first and I learned how to host one from Fred McCall, who started the one at Campbell. They would take over the whole campus for their summer camps. Among my counselors were pros like Dave Cowens, Rudy Tomjanovich, and Pete Maravich, and kids that came included future stars like Mike Giminski, Johnny Dawkins, Tommy Amaker, and Danny Ferry when they were eight- and nine-year-olds.

On His Assistant Coaches: "I was blessed with some great assistant coaches through the years, including many who went on to become college head coaches. From Davidson, Warren Mitchell went on to be the head coach at William & Mary, Gale Catlett went on to coach Cincinnati and West Virginia, and Terry Holland took over at Davidson and later Virginia. From Maryland, George Raveling became head coach at Washington State, Iowa, and Southern Cal; Joe Harrington went on to coach Hofstra, Long Beach State, George Mason, and Colorado; Dave Pritchett coached Davidson; Will Jones coached the University of the District of Columbia; Tom Abedomarco coached Radford and Old Dominion; Ron Bradley coached Radford; John

Kochan coached Millersville; and Oliver Purnell coached Dayton, Clemson, and most recently DePaul. Chuck, who was my assistant at James Madison, has obviously been at The Citadel; Mike Perry was with me at Georgia State before becoming the head coach there; and Travis Williams, who was with me for a couple of years at Georgia State, has since been the head coach at Tennessee State (also, Phil Cunningham has since become head coach at Troy University). Others who applied for my assistant jobs that I probably should have hired included Mike Fratello (Atlanta Hawks), "Tubby" Smith (Tulsa, Georgia, Kentucky, Minnesota, and Texas Tech), and Rick Barnes (Clemson and University of Texas). When I think about those names, I don't feel so smart."

On His Basketball Banquets: "Nobody had better speakers at their season-ending basketball banquets than I did at Maryland. While I was there, we had speakers like Al McGuire, Jesse Owens, John Wooden, "Red" Auerbach, Adolph Rupp, Bill Russell, and Mohammed Ali. Let's see anybody top that."

On Basketball's Biggest Changes During His Lifetime: "I have seen a lot of them—like going from the small lane to the larger one, the advent of the jump shot, the three-point shot, and alternating possessions, but undoubtedly the biggest change was the influx and dominance of African-American players, starting in the 1960s. 'The Big O,' Oscar Robertson (University of Cincinnati), was the first black player I ever saw play in the South. That was against Duke in the old Dixie Classic."

On His Coaching Heroes: "That's easy…John Wooden, "Red" Auerbach, and one that might surprise you—Frank Howard, the old Clemson University football coach."

Please Note: All preceding epilogue comments by Charles "Lefty" Driesell from interviews with the author, November 2012.

Appendix I

On 7 April 2014, Gary Williams was named to the Naismith Memorial Basketball Hall of Fame. That honor came just a week after he also earned Collegiate Basketball Hall of Fame recognition. It was a quick and supreme first ballot double dip for the coach with his name on the University of Maryland basketball court.

Whether or not the ascension of one former Maryland head coach to the Naismith Hall will preclude another from getting there remains to be seen, but a quick comparison of their careers at UM makes the case for "Lefty" even stronger. Obviously, Williams's national championship team in 2002 undoubtedly put him over the top, but consider:

—While Gary Williams won 64 percent of his games at Maryland between 1990 and 2010, "Lefty" Driesell captured 68 percent of his between 1970 and 1986.

—While both enjoyed winning percentages of 55 percent in ACC play, Coach Williams won only 47 percent of his games in the ACC Tournament, while Coach Driesell won at a 53 percent rate in the nation's oldest and most prestigious conference tourney.

—Both captured one ACC Tournament title, but while Williams reached the ACC Finals twice, "Lefty" got his teams there six times in five less tries.

—In fact, while Driesell enjoyed a winning conference record in 11 of his 17 seasons at the Maryland helm, Williams was on the winning side of the ACC ledger in just 10 of his 22.

—Both were voted ACC Coach-of-the-Year twice, but while Williams posted five national Top Ten finishes in 22 years, "Lefty's" teams finished in the Top Ten six times in 17 years.

—Also, while Williams endured two losing seasons at Maryland, Driesell had none; while Williams produced 22 first or second team all-conference players, "Lefty" developed 27; and due in large part to the promotional magic created by such things as Midnight Madness, Driesell's teams led the ACC in attendance for 15 straight seasons while winning more ACC games during that time than any other conference team except North Carolina.

—And finally, while "Lefty" Driesell won 786 games at four different schools, only one of which (Maryland) was a member of a power conference, Gary Williams won over 100 less (668), also at four, three of which were members of power conferences (Boston College, Ohio State, and Maryland).

Please Note: Source, the University of Maryland Men's Basketball Online History.

Appendix II

"Lefty's" College Coaching Record

Season	School	W	L	Pct.	(Final Ranking)
1960–1961	Davidson	9	14	.391	
1961–1962	Davidson	14	11	.560	
1962–1963	Davidson	20	7	.741	
1963–1964	Davidson	22	4	.846	(10th AP, 10th UPI)
1964–1965	Davidson	24	2	.923	(6th AP, 7th UPI)
1965–1966	Davidson	21	7	.750	(18th UPI)
1966–1967	Davidson	15	12	.556	
1967–1968	Davidson	24	5	.828	(8th AP, 9th UPI)
1968–1969	Davidson	27	3	.900	(5th AP, 3rd UPI)
1969–1970	Maryland	13	13	.500	
1970–1971	Maryland	14	12	.538	
1971–1972	Maryland	27	5	.844	(14th AP, 11th UPI)
1972–1973	Maryland	23	7	.767	(8th AP, 10th, UPI)
1973–1974	Maryland	23	5	.821	(4th AP, 4th UPI)
1974–1975	Maryland	24	5	.828	(5th AP, 5th UPI)
1975–1976	Maryland	22	6	.786	(11th AP, 13th UPI)

1976–1977	Maryland	19	8	.704	
1977–1978	Maryland	15	13	.536	
1978–1979	Maryland	19	11	.633	
1979–1980	Maryland	24	7	.744	(8th AP, 8th UPI)
1980–1981	Maryland	21	10	.677	(18th AP, 20th UPI)
1981–1982	Maryland	16	13	.552	
1982–1983	Maryland	20	10	.667	
1983–1984	Maryland	24	8	.750	(11th AP, 10th UPI)
1984–1985	Maryland	25	12	.676	
1985–1986	Maryland	19	14	.576	
1988–1989	James Madison	16	14	.533	
1989–1990	James Madison	20	11	.645	
1990–1991	James Madison	19	10	.655	
1991–1992	James Madison	21	11	.656	
1992–1993	James Madison	21	9	.700	
1993–1994	James Madison	20	10	.667	
1994–1995	James Madison	16	13	.552	
1995–1996	James Madison	10	20	.333	
1996–1997	James Madison	16	13	.542	
1997–1998	Georgia State	16	12	.571	
1998–1999	Georgia State	17	13	.567	
1999–2000	Georgia State	17	12	.586	
2000–2001	Georgia State	29	5	.853	(32nd)
2001–2002	Georgia State	20	11	.645	
TOTALS	41 YEARS	786	394	.644	

"Lefty's" Conference Champions

1963–1964	Southern Conference (Season)
1964–1965	Southern Conference (Season)
1965–1966	Southern Conference (Season)
1965–1966	Southern Conference (Tournament)
1967–1968	Southern Conference (Season)
1968–1969	Southern Conference (Tournament)
1974–1975	Atlantic Coast Conference (Season)
1979–1980	Atlantic Coast Conference (Season)
1983–1984	Atlantic Coast Conference (Tournament)
1989–1990	Colonial Athletic Conference (Season)
1990–1991	Colonial Athletic Conference (Season)
1991–1992	Colonial Athletic Conference (Season)
1992–1993	Colonial Athletic Conference (Season)
1993–1994	Colonial Athletic Conference (Season)
1993–1994	Colonial Athletic Conference (Tournament)
1999–2000	Trans America Athletic Conference (Season Co-Champ)
2000–2001	Trans America Athletic Conference (Season)
2000–2001	Trans America Athletic Conference (Tournament)
2001–2002	Atlantic Sun Conference (Season Co-Champ)

"Lefty's" Best Teams
BY WINS

29 Wins (5 Losses)	Georgia State (2000–2001)
27 Wins (3 Losses)	Davidson (1968–1969)
27 Wins (5 Losses)	Maryland (1971–1972)
25 Wins (12 Losses)	Maryland (1984–1985)
24 Wins (2 Losses)	Davidson (1964–1965)
24 Wins (5 Losses)	Davidson (1967–1968)
24 Wins (5 Losses)	Maryland (1974–1975)
24 Wins (7 Losses)	Maryland (1979–1980)

24 Wins (8 Losses)	Maryland (1983–1984)
23 Wins (5 Losses)	Maryland (1973–1974)
23 Wins (7 Losses)	Maryland (1972–1973)
22 Wins (4 Losses)	Davidson (1963–1964)
22 Wins (6 Losses)	Maryland (1975–1976)
21 Wins (7 Losses)	Davidson (1965–1966)
21 Wins (9 Losses)	James Madison (1992–1993)
21 Wins (10 Losses)	Maryland (1980–1981)
21 Wins (11 Losses)	James Madison (1991–1992)

BY FINAL RANKING (Wire Service)

3rd (UPI)	Davidson (1968–1969)
4th (AP & UPI)	Maryland (1973–1974)
5th (AP & UPI)	Maryland (1974–1975)
5th (AP)	Davidson (1968–1969)
6th (AP)	Davidson (1964–1965)
7th (UPI)	Davidson (1964–1965)
8th (AP & UPI)	Maryland (1979–1980)
8th (AP)	Davidson (1967–1968)
10th (AP & UPI)	Davidson (1963–1964)
10th (UPI)	Davidson (1967–1968)
10th (UPI)	Maryland (1983–1984)
11th (AP)	Maryland (1983–1984)
11th (AP)	Maryland (1975–1976)
11th (UPI)	Maryland (1971–1972)
13th (UPI)	Maryland (1975–1976)
14th (AP)	Maryland (1971–1972)
18th (AP)	Maryland (1980–1981)
20th (UPI)	Maryland (1980–1981)

"Lefty's" First-Team All-Americans

Player	School	Year
Fred Hetzel	Davidson	1965
Dick Snyder	Davidson	1966
Mike Malloy	Davidson	1969
Tom McMillen	Maryland	1974
Len Elmore	Maryland	1974
John Lucas	Maryland	1976
Brad Davis	Maryland	1977
Albert King	Maryland	1981
Buck Williams	Maryland	1981
Len Bias	Maryland	1986

"Lefty's" First-Round Draft Picks

Player	NBA Team	Year
Fred Hetzel	San Francisco	1965
Mike Malloy	Pittsburgh	1970
Tom McMillen	Buffalo	1974
Len Elmore	Washington	1974
John Lucas	Houston	1976
Brad Davis	Los Angeles	1977
Buck Williams	New Jersey	1981
Albert King	New Jersey	1981
Len Bias	Boston	1986

"Lefty's" Milestone College Wins

1st Win – Davidson 65, Wake Forest 59 (1960–1961, age 28)

100th – Davidson 105, West Virginia 79 (1965–1966, age 34)

200th – Maryland 88, Loyola (Md.) 69 (1970–1971, age 39)

300th – Maryland 83, Notre Dame 71 (1974–1975, age 43)

400th – Maryland 86, Navy 64 (1980–1981, age 49)

500th – Maryland 91, Towson State 38 (1984–1985, age 53)

600th – James Madison 81, American 57 (1991–1992, age 60)

700th – Georgia State 84, North Florida 74 (1998–1999, age 67)

750th – Georgia State 86, Mercer 77 (2001–2002, age 69)

Last – Georgia State 73, Furman 62 (2002–2003, age 72)

"Lefty's" Wins by Presidential Administration

President	Wins	Party
Dwight Eisenhower	6	Republican
John Kennedy	37	Democrat
Lyndon Johnson	122	Democrat
Richard Nixon	111	Republican
Gerald Ford	58	Republican
Jimmy Carter	77	Democrat
Ronald Reagan	123	Republican
George Bush	77	Republican
Bill Clinton	137	Democrat
George W. Bush	38	Republican
TOTALS	786	413 Republican / 373 Democrat

Source: *2002–2003 Georgia State Basketball Fact Book* (updated), 22–37.

Selected Bibliography

Beeler, Joey, Marc Gignac, and John Kilgo. *Davidson 2012–2013 Men's Basketball Media Guide*. Moorsville NC: Cover2Group, 2012.

Bolno, Zack. "Maryland Men's Basketball Digital Media Guide." College Park MD: University of Maryland Athletics Media Relations, 2012.

Bowers, Matt, and Steve Kirschner. *Carolina Basketball 2012–2013*. Chapel Hill NC: University Directories, 2012.

Bozich, Rick. "Knight Headed Beyond 880, If Knight Doesn't Get in Way." *Basketball Times* (March 2003): 17.

Coffin, Judy. "The Professionals." *Charlotte Magazine* (July–August 1977): 34.

Colson, Bob. "50 from 50." *Sports Illustrated* (December 1999): 11, 96.

Driesell, Charles G. "Graduation Patterns of Male Student Athletes Initially Enrolled in the Years 1974–1979." Memorandum to Dr. John Slaughter, Chancellor, and Members of the Maryland Board of Regents (11 August 1986).

———. Personal letter to Dr. John B. Slaughter, Chancellor, University of Maryland (4 September 1986).

———. Personal letter to Dr. John B. Slaughter, Chancellor, University of Maryland (16 September 1986).

Elfin, David. "Driesell Deserves Spot in Real Hall of Fame." WJFK-The Fan Blog (11 October 2011).

Feinstein, John. *Last Dance: Behind the Scenes at the Final Four*. New York & Boston: Little Brown & Company, 2006.

Fraser, Kirk. "Without Bias." Owensboro KY: ESPN Films (2010).

Gigmac, Marc. "Lefty's Legacy." *Davidson Journal* (17 March 2011): 22.

Gleason, Joshua. "Travis Williams's Difficult Route to Being Division I Head Coach." *Bleacher Report* (6 May 2013), http://bleacherreport.com (accessed May 2013).

Harmon, Martin. Original nomination letter for Charles "Lefty" Driesell to Naismith Memorial Basketball Hall of Fame selection committee (10 January 2000).

Holliday, Johnny, with Stephen Moore. *Hoop Tales: Maryland Terrapins Men's Basketball*. Guilford CT: Morris Book Publishing, 2007.

Inter Fraternity Council. Award of appreciation to Charles G. "Lefty" Driesell (1986).

Jessop, Alicia. "The Business of NCAA Basketball Midnight Madness." *Forbes* (12 October 2012).

Jones, Bomani. "Len Bias Gone, but Not Forgotten." ESPN Page 2 (6 June 2006).

Kirkpatrick, Curry. "Something's Gotta Give." *Sports Illustrated* (29 November 1982): 87.

Martin, John A., Gary Michael, and Kevin Warner. *2012–2013 James Madison University Men's Basketball Media Guide*. Harrisonburg VA: JMU Multimedia Communications, 2012.

Maryland House of Delegates. Resolution of congratulations to "Lefty" Driesell (2 March 1987).

Maryland State Senate. Resolution of congratulations to "Lefty" Driesell (2 March 1987).

McMillen, Tom, with Paul Coggins. *Out of Bounds*. New York: Simon & Schuster, 1992.

McMullen, Paul. *Maryland Basketball: Tales from Cole Fieldhouse*. Baltimore: John Hopkins University Press, 2002.

Morehead, Phillip. *New American Roget's College Thesaurus*. New York: The Penguin Group, 1985.

"Naismith Memorial Basketball Hall of Fame." http://hoophall.com/halloffamers (accessed December 2012).

Neff, Craig, and Bruce Selcraig. "One Shock Wave after Another." *Sports Illustrated* (10 November 1986): 76–93.

Novak, Robert D. *The Prince of Darkness*. New York: Crown Forum, 2007.

Olson, Lute. "Among the Many Words That Describe 'Lefty,' the Best Would Be 'Genuine.'" *Basketball Times* (March 2003): 41.

"Press Conference – Charles 'Lefty' Driesell." *Basketball Times* (March 2003): 10–12.

Scott, Charles. Davidson College Letter of Intent (1 October 1965).

Slaughter, John B. "Bringing Excellence to College Park." Farewell remarks to Campus Senate as University of Maryland Chancellor (1988).

Smith, C. Fraser. "The Education of John Slaughter." *Regardie's* (March 1988): 96–98, 101–105, 136–44.

———. *Lenny, "Lefty," and the Chancellor*. Baltimore: The Bancroft Press, 1992.

Smith, Dean E. Letter of support for "Lefty" Driesell's Naismith Memorial Hall of Fame candidacy to Senator Russ Potts (10 November 2004).

Sport Staff Report. "Hardwood Huckster." *Time* (22 January 1973): 41.

Taylor, Charlie. *2002–2003 Georgia State Basketball Fact Book*. Atlanta: Georgia State University, 2002.

Thomas, Evan. *The Man to See*. New York: Simon & Schuster, 1991.

Thompson, John. "John Thompson on 'Lefty' Driesell." ESPN Radio (2 February 2012).

Treadwell, Sandy. "Give 'Lefty' A V, A V and…." *Sports Illustrated* (25 January 1971): 42.

Ungrady, Dave. *Born Ready: The Mixed Legacy of Len Bias*. New York: CreateSpace Independent Publishing Platform, 2011.

———. *Legends of Maryland Basketball*. Champaign IL: Sports Publishing, 2004.

Wills, Denise Kersten. "45 Who Shaped Washington, 1965–2010." *Washingtonian* (October 2010): 78.

Wortman, Scott. *Wake Forest Basketball 2012–2013 Media Guide.* Winston-Salem NC: Keys Printing, 2012.

Source Newspapers

Atlanta Journal/Constitution
Baltimore Sun
Boston Herald
Charlotte Observer
Greensboro News & Record
The GSU Signal
Hampton Roads Daily Press
Harrisonburg (VA) Daily News
Kansas City Star
Los Angeles Times
Montgomery Advertiser
Norfolk Ledger-Dispatch
Philadelphia Inquirer
USA Today
The Virginian-Pilot
Washington (NC) Daily News
Washington Post
Washington Star
Washington Times

Author Interviews (with relationship to subject)

Anthony, Leo. Former Granby High School basketball star under Coach "Lefty" Driesell, by telephone (6 February 2013).

Branch, Adrian. Former University of Maryland basketball star under Coach "Lefty" Driesell, by telephone (5 March 2013).

Britt, Jim. Former James Madison University radio play-by-play announcer when "Lefty" Driesell was JMU head coach, by telephone (2 April 2013).

Brown, Johnny. Former coach and teacher at Granby High School when "Lefty" Driesell began coaching career, by telephone (25 January 2013).

Butler, Dan. Former University of Tennessee football star and high-school friend of "Lefty" Driesell, by telephone (17 February 2013).

Chambers, Bill. Former Virginia high school basketball coach and semi-pro teammate of "Lefty" Driesell, by telephone (18 January 2013).

Cohen, Dave. Radio play-by-play announcer for Georgia State University basketball, including period when "Lefty" Driesell was coach, in person in Atlanta, Georgia (11 April 2013).

Driesell, Charles "Lefty." College Hall of Fame basketball coach and subject of biography, in person at Virginia Beach VA (15–19 November 2012).

Driesell, Joyce. Wife of Coach "Lefty" Driesell, in person at Virginia Beach VA (17–18 November 2012).

Groat, Dick. Former Duke University basketball star and teammate of "Lefty" Driesell, by telephone (18 January 2013).

Harrington, Joe. Former University of Maryland assistant basketball coach under "Lefty" Driesell, by e-mail (17 February 2013).

Hetzel, Fred. Former Davidson College basketball star under Coach "Lefty" Driesell, by telephone (29 January 2013).

Holland, Terry. Former Davidson College basketball star and assistant coach under "Lefty" Driesell, by e-mail (6 February 2013).

Huckel, Wayne. Former Davidson College basketball star under Coach "Lefty" Driesell, by telephone (4 February 2013).

Malone, Moses. Former Virginia prep basketball star recruited and signed by "Lefty" Driesell, by telephone (27 February 2013).

Martin, D. G. Former Davidson College player (and son of college president) under Coach "Lefty" Driesell, by telephone (7 February 2013).

Packer, Billy. Former Wake Forest University basketball star and longtime NCAA basketball TV commentator, by telephone (28 January 2013).

Perry, Michael. Former Georgia State University assistant basketball coach under "Lefty" Driesell, by telephone (22 April 2013).

Potts, Russ. Former University of Maryland athletics promotions director and Virginia state senator, by telephone (29 March 2013).

Radcliffe, Martha. Sister of "Lefty" Driesell, by telephone (17 December 2012).

Schuh, Cameron. NCAA Enforcement representative, by telephone (14 March 2013).

Scott, Charlie. Former North Carolina prep basketball star recruited and signed by "Lefty" Driesell, by telephone (3 February 2013).

Teague, Barry. Former Davidson College basketball star under Coach "Lefty" Driesell, by telephone (3 January 2013).

White, Howard. Former University of Maryland basketball star and assistant coach under "Lefty" Driesell, by telephone (6 March 2013).

Notes

[1] Lute Olson, "Among the Many Words that Describe 'Lefty,' the Best Would Be Genuine," *Basketball Times* (March 2003): 41.

[2] Phillip Morehead, ed., *The New American Roget's College Thesaurus* (New York: The Penguin Group, 1985) 318.

[3] "Lefty" Driesell, interviews with the author, Virginia Beach VA (15–19 November 2012).

[4] C. Fraser Smith, *Lenny, "Lefty," and the Chancellor* (Baltimore: The Bancroft Press, 1992) 115.

[5] Ibid., 118–19. Also, Dave Ungrady, *Born Ready: The Mixed Legacy of Len Bias* (New York: CreateSpace Independent Publishing Platform, 2011) 53; and "Lefty" Driesell, interviews (15–19 November 2012).

[6] Johnny Holliday with Stephen Moore, *Hoop Tales: Maryland Terrapins Men's Basketball* (Guilford CT: Morris Book Publishing, 2007) 102.

[7] Charlie Taylor, *2002–2003 Georgia State Basketball Fact Book* (Atlanta: Georgia State University, 2002) 29–37.

[8] "Driesell Among Inductees to College Hoops Hall of Fame," *The Virginian-Pilot* (3 April 2007): Sports 1; and David Boyce, "Coach a Master Motivator," *Kansas City Star* (19 November 2007): CC2.

[9] Wikipedia, "Ed Diddle," "Marv Harshman," "Ralph Miller," "Lou Carneseca," "Pete Carril," and "John Chaney," http://enwikipedia.org (accessed December 2012).

[10] Naismith Memorial Basketball Hall of Fame official website, "History" and "Inductees," http://hoophall.com/history (accessed December 2012).

[11] Ibid.

[12] John Feinstein, "In Conclusion, 'Lefty' Had the Right Stuff," *Washington Post* (4 January 2003): D8; David Elfin, "Driesell Deserves Spot in Real Hall of Fame," WJFK-The Fan Blog (11 October 2011); and Paul McMullen, *Maryland Basketball: Tales from Cole Field House* (Baltimore: John Hopkins University Press, 2002) 109.

[13] John Feinstein, *Last Dance: Behind the Scenes at the Final Four* (New York & Boston: Little Brown & Company, 2006) 149–53; and John Feinstein, "It's Past Time to Recognize 'Lefty,'" *Washington Post* (21 October 2008) http://washingtonpost.com (accessed March 2013).

[14] Bob Molinaro, "Good Tidings and Cheer for the Naughty Nice of Sports," *The Virginian-Pilot* (17 December 2008): Sports 1; Dave Fairbank, "Hall Isn't Complete Without 'Lefty,'" *Hampton Roads Daily Press* (30 March 2005): B1, B5; Jeff Schultz, "'Lefty' Out of Hall? 'Lefty's' Too Good," *Atlanta Journal/Constitution* (19 March 2003): C4; and (also Jeff Schultz) "Hall's Snub of Driesell a Shame," *Atlanta Journal/Constitution* (20 April 2014): C10.

[15] Jeff Zillgitt, "Exclusion of Miller Sparks Hall Debate," *USA Today* (21 February 2011): 5C.

[16] Martin Harmon, follow-up e-mail request to Jen Gray (25 February 2013).

[17] "Lefty" Driesell, interviews (15–19 November 2012); and Cameron Schuh, interview with the author by telephone (14 March 2013).

[18] Wikipedia, "Jerry Tarkanian" and "Eddie Sutton," http://enwikipedia.org (accessed December 2012).

[19] Kirk Frazier, "Without Bias" (Owensboro KY: ESPN Films, 2010) interview with Michael Wilbon; and McMullen, *Maryland Basketball: Tales from Cole Field House,* 106.

[20] Wikipedia, "Len Bias," http://enwikipedia.org (accessed December 2012).

[21] C. Fraser Smith, *Lenny, "Lefty," and the Chancellor,* 35.

[22] Ibid., 36.

[23] Ungrady, *Born Ready: The Mixed Legacy of Len Bias,* 46–177.

[24] Ibid., 59. Also, "Lefty" Driesell, interviews (15–19 November 2012).

[25] Wikipedia, "Bill Buckner" and "Jackie Smith," http://enwikipedia.org (accessed December 2012).

[26] Wikipedia, "Bob Knight," http://enwikipedia.org (accessed December 2012); and Rick Bozich, "Knight Headed Beyond 880, If Knight Doesn't Get in Way," *Basketball Times* (March 2003): 17.

[27] Wikipedia, "John Chaney," http://enwikipedia.org (accessed December 2012).

[28] Dean E. Smith, Letter to Virginia State Senator Russ Potts (10 November 2004).

[29] Robyn Norwood, "Driesell Shouldn't Be Left Behind," *Los Angeles Times* (9 January 2003): C3.

[30] John Thompson, "John Thompson on 'Lefty' Driesell," ESPN Radio transcript (27 February 2012).

[31] Olson, "Among the Many Words that Describe 'Lefty,'" 41.

[32] Doug Roberson, "'Lefty' Still Hoping for Call from Hall of Fame," *Atlanta Journal/Constitution* (24 January 2013): C8.

[33] Jeff Barker, "Maryland to Honor 'Lefty' Driesell with Bronze Relief, Sources Say," *Baltimore Sun* (11 February 2013): Sports 3.

[34] Wikipedia, "Jerry Tarkanian," "Guy Lewis," and "Rick Pitino," http://enwikipedia.org (accessed May 2013).

[35] "Lefty" Driesell, interviews (15–19 November 2012).

[36] "Driesell," http://ancestry.com (accessed 19 November 2012).

[37] "Lefty" Driesell, interviews (15–19 November 2012); and "Death of Frank Driesell, Veteran Jeweler of Norfolk, Va., Passes Away after Long Career," *The Virginian-Pilot* (20 June 1914).

[38] "Lefty" Driesell, interviews (15–19 November 2012).

[39] Ibid.

[40] Ibid. Also, Martha Radcliffe, interview with the author by telephone (17 December 2012).

[41] "Lefty" Driesell, interviews (15–19 November 2012).

[42] Radcliffe, interview (17 December 2012).

[43] Ibid.

[44] "Lefty" Driesell, interviews (15–19 November 2012).

[45] Radcliffe, interview (17 December 2012).

[46] Ibid.

[47] "Lefty" Driesell, interviews (15–19 November 2012).

[48] Ibid.

[49] Ibid.

[50] "Lefty" Driesell, interviews (15–19 November 2012).

[51] Dan Butler, interview with the author by telephone (17 February 2013).

[52] "Lefty" Driesell, interviews (15–19 November 2012).

[53] Dick Groat, interview with the author by telephone (18 January 2013).

[54] "Lefty" Driesell, interviews (15–19 November 2012); and Wikipedia, "Jack Lucas," http://enwikipedia.org (accessed January 2013).

[55] Ibid.

[56] "1933 Ford Roadster," Kelly Blue Book, http://kellybluebook.com (accessed 1 May 2013).

[57] "Lefty" Driesell, interviews (15–19 November 2012).

[58] Ibid.

[59] Ibid.

[60] GoDuke.com, "Duke Blue Devils Basketball Statistical Database," http://goduke.statsgeek.com/basketball (accessed December 2012); and "Lefty" Driesell, interviews (15–19 November 2012).

[61] Ibid.

[62] Joyce Driesell, interviews with the author, Virginia Beach VA (17–18 November 2012).

[63] "Lefty" Driesell, interviews (15–19 November 2012).

[64] Ibid.

[65] Ibid.

[66] Ibid.

[67] Ibid.

[68] Johnny Brown, interview with the author by telephone (25 January 2013).

[69] "Lefty" Driesell, interviews (15–19 November 2012).

[70] Ibid. Also, Sport Staff Report, "Hardwood Huckster," *Time* (22 January 1973): 41.

[71] "Lefty" Driesell, interviews (15–19 November 2012); Wayne Woodlief, "Driesell Sets City Cage Record," *Norfolk Ledger-Dispatch* (December 1955); and "Driesell as Good as Anybody, Says Buzzy Wilkinson," *Norfolk Ledger-Dispatch* (March 1956).

[72] "Lefty" Driesell, interviews (15–19 November 2012).

[73] "Lefty" Driesell, interviews (15–19 November 2012).

[74] Leo Anthony, interview with the author by telephone (6 February 2013).

[75] Bill Chambers, interview with the author by telephone (18 January 2013).

[76] Dave Fairbank, "'Lefty's' Typhoon Was the Perfect Storm," *Hampton Roads Daily Press* (18 May 2008).

[77] "Lefty" Driesell, interviews (15–19 November 2012).

[78] Ibid.

[79] Ibid.

[80] Joey Beeler, Marc Gignac, and John Kilgo, *Davidson 2012–2013 Men's Basketball Media Guide* (Moorsville NC: Cover2Group, 2012): 86.

[81] "Lefty" Driesell, interviews (15–19 November 2012); and Treadwell, "Give 'Lefty' A V, A V And…," 42.

[82] Billy Packer, interview with the author by telephone (28 January 2013).

[83] D. G. Martin, interview with the author by telephone (7 February 2013).

[84] "Lefty" Driesell, interviews (15–19 November 2012); and Sport Staff Report, "Hardwood Huckster," 41.

[85] Terry Holland, interview with the author by e-mail (6 February 2013).

[86] "Lefty" Driesell interviews (15–19 November 2012); and Sport Staff Report, "Hardwood Huckster," 41.

[87] "Lefty" Driesell, interviews (15–19 November 2012).

[88] Ibid.

[89] Beeler, Gignac, and Kilgo, *Davidson 2012–2013 Men's Basketball Media Guide,* 90–91.

[90] Barry Teague, interview with the author by telephone (13 January 2013).

[91] "Lefty" Driesell, interviews (15–19 November 2012).

[92] Beeler, Gignac, and Kilgo, *Davidson 2012–2013 Men's Basketball Media Guide,* 120–21.

[93] "Lefty" Driesell, interviews (15–19 November 2012).

[94] Beeler, Gignac, and Kilgo, *Davidson 2012–2013 Men's Basketball Media Guide,* 92–93, 103, 106.

[95] Fred Hetzel, interview with the author by telephone (29 January 2013).

[96] Ibid.

[97] Beeler, Gignac, and Kilgo, *Davidson 2012–2013 Men's Basketball Media Guide,* 120–21.

[98] "Lefty" Driesell, interviews (15–19 November 2012).

[99] Wikipedia, "NCAA Basketball Championship Games," http://enwikipedia.com (accessed 1 February 2013).

[100] "Lefty" Driesell, interviews (15–19 November 2012).

[101] "Davidson 10th in Final Poll," *The Associated Press* (March 1964).

[102] "Lefty" Driesell, interviews (15–19 November 2012).

[103] Teague, interview (3 January 2013).

[104] "Lefty" Driesell, interviews (15–19 November 2012).

[105] Beeler, Gignac, and Kilgo, *Davidson 2012–2013 Men's Basketball Media Guide,* 92–93.

[106] Teague, interview (3 January 2013).

[107] "Lefty" Driesell, interviews (15–19 November 2012).

[108] Beeler, Gignac, and Kilgo, *Davidson 2012–2013 Men's Basketball Media Guide,* 91; and "Lefty" Driesell, interviews (15–19 November 2012).

[109] Mel Derrick, "Negro Cage Star Applies for Admission to Davidson," *Charlotte Observer* (October 1965).

[110] Charles Scott, interview with the author by telephone (3 February 2013).

[111] Matt Bowers and Steve Kirschner, *Carolina Basketball 2012–2013* (Chapel Hill NC: University Directories, 2012) 187–91.

[112] Scott, interview (3 February 2013).

[113] Ibid.

[114] Mel Derrick, "Negro Cage Star Applies for Admission to Davidson," *Charlotte Observer* 2C.

[115] Gene Warren, "Scott Explains Why He Picked Carolina," *Washington (NC) Daily News* (Summer 1966).

[116] "Lefty" Driesell, interviews (15–19 November 2012).

[117] Beeler, Gignac, and Kilgo, *Davidson 2012–2013 Men's Basketball Media Guide,* 99, 121, 152–53; and "Lefty" Driesell, interviews (15–19 November 2012).

[118] Wayne Huckel, interview with the author by telephone (4 February 2013).

[119] Beeler, Gignac, and Kilgo, *Davidson 2012–2013 Men's Basketball Media Guide,* 90–91, 152–53.

[120] Huckel, interview (4 February 2013).

[121] "Lefty" Driesell, interviews (15–19 November 2012).

[122] "Davidson Is Eighth in Final Press Poll," *The Associated Press* (March 1968); and "Wildcats Are Third in Final Press Poll," *The Associated Press* (March 1969).

[123] Bowers and Kirschner, *Carolina Basketball 2012–2013,* 129, 138.

[124] Huckel, interview (4 February 2013).

[125] "Lefty" Driesell, interviews (15–19 November 2012).

[126] Holland, interview (6 February 2013).

[127] Huckel, interview (4 February 2013); and Wikipedia, "Mike Maloy," http://enwikipedia.org (accessed 14 April 2013); and David Boraks, "Former Wildcat Star Mike Maloy Dies in Vienna," DavidsonNews.net, http://davidsonnews.net/blog (accessed May 2013).

[128] "Lefty" Driesell, interviews (15–19 November 2012); and Huckel, interview (4 February 2013).

[129] Zack Bolno, "Maryland Men's Basketball Digital Media Guide" (College Park MD: University of Maryland Athletics Media Relations, 2012).

[130] Ibid.

[131] Packer, interview (28 January 2013).

[132] Bolno, "Maryland Men's Basketball Digital Media Guide," 196; and "Lefty" Driesell, interviews (15–19 November 2012).

[133] Ibid.

[134] Ibid.

---

[135] James H. Jackson, "Driesell Plans 'UCLA Look' for Maryland," *Baltimore Sun* (March 1969); and Treadwell, "Give 'Lefty' A V, A V And…," 42.

[136] "Lefty" Driesell, interviews (15–19 November 2012).

[137] Ibid.

[138] Taylor, *2002–2003 Georgia State Basketball Fact Book,* 34.

[139] Joe Harrington, interview with the author by e-mail (17 February 2013).

[140] Ibid.

[141] "Lefty" Driesell, interviews (15–19 November 2012); McMullen, *Maryland Basketball: Tales from Cole Field House,* 52–53; and Treadwell, "Give 'Lefty' A V, A V And…," 42.

[142] "Lefty" Driesell, interviews (15–19 November 2012); Sport Staff Report, "Hardwood Huckster," 41; and McMullen, *Maryland Basketball: Tales from Cole Field House,* 56–63.

[143] Ibid.

[144] Ibid.

[145] Holliday with Moore, *Hoop Tales: Maryland Terrapins Men's Basketball,* 21; and Treadwell, "Give 'Lefty' A V, A V And…," 42.

[146] Robert D. Novak, *The Prince of Darkness* (New York: Crown Forum, 2007) 201–202.

[147] "Lefty" Driesell, interviews (15–19 November 2012).

[148] Dave Ungrady, *Legends of Maryland Basketball* (Champaign IL: Sports Publishing, 2004) 36–39, 42–45.

[149] Alicia Jessop, "The Business of NCAA Basketball Midnight Madness," *Forbes* (12 October 2012) http://forbes.com (accessed April 2013).

[150] Tom McMillen with Paul Coggins, *Out of Bounds* (New York: Simon & Schuster, 1992) 99; and Ungrady, *Legends of Maryland Basketball,* 36–39, 42–45.

[151] Jessop, "The Business of NCAA Basketball Midnight Madness" (accessed April 2013).

[152] File Photo, University of Maryland Athletics Media Relations (15 October 1971).

[153] Jessop, "The Business of NCAA Basketball Midnight Madness" (accessed April 2013); and "Lefty" Driesell, interviews (15–19 November 2012).

[154] Ibid.

[155] Ibid.

[156] Ibid.

[157] McMillen with Coggins, *Out of Bounds,* 56.

[158] "Lefty" Driesell, interviews (15–19 November 2012).

[159] Ibid.

[160] Bolno, "Maryland Men's Basketball Digital Media Guide," 158, 188; and McMullen, *Maryland Basketball: Tales from Cole Field House,* 64–73.

[161] Bolno, "Maryland Men's Basketball Digital Media Guide," 158.

[162] Peter Carry, "If You Want Tom, Easy Does It," *Sports Illustrated* (14 February 1970).

[163] McMillen with Coggins, *Out of Bounds,* 35; and Bolno, "Maryland Men's Basketball Digital Media Guide," 189.

[164] Ungrady, *Legends of Maryland Basketball,* 36–39; and Bolno, "Maryland Men's Basketball Digital Media Guide," 189, 202.

[165] Ibid. Also, Ungrady, *Legends of Maryland Basketball,* 42–45.

[166] Dick Heller, "Still the Greatest Game Ever Played," *Washington Times* (8 March 2004).

[167] McMullen, *Maryland Basketball: Tales from Cole Field House,* 64–73; and McMillen with Coggins, *Out of Bounds,* 160.

[168] "Lefty" Driesell, interviews (15–19 November 2012).

[169] Wikipedia, "NCAA Award of Valor," http://enwikipedia.org (accessed February 2013); "Award of Valor," http://ncaa.org (accessed February 2013); and "Lefty" Driesell, interviews (15–19 November 2012).

[170] Ibid.

[171] Ungrady, *Legends of Maryland Basketball,* 49.

[172] Bolno, "Maryland Men's Basketball Digital Media Guide," 189, 202; and Wikipedia, "John Lucas," http://enwikipedia.org (accessed February 2012).

[173] Ibid.

[174] McMillen with Coggins, *Out of Bounds,* 161.

[175] Holliday with Moore, *Hoop Tales: Maryland Terrapins Men's Basketball,* 85; and Ungrady, *Legends of Maryland Basketball,* 51.

[176] McMullen, *Maryland Basketball: Tales from Cole Field House,* 75–76; and Bolno, "Maryland Men's Basketball Digital Media Guide," 188.

[177] Wikipedia, "Brad Davis," http://enwikipedia.org (accessed February 2012); and "Lefty" Driesell, interviews (15–19 November 2012).

[178] Bolno, "Maryland Men's Basketball Digital Media Guide," 195.

[179] Ungrady, *Legends of Maryland Basketball,* 57.

[180] Ibid., 54–55.

[181] Howard White, interview with author by telephone (6 March 2013).

[182] McMullen, *Maryland Basketball: Tales from Cole Field House,* 74–82.

¹⁸³ Ibid., 75–76.

¹⁸⁴ Bolno, "Maryland Men's Basketball Digital Media Guide," 188, 195; and "Lefty" Driesell, interviews (15–19 November 2012).

¹⁸⁵ Ibid.

¹⁸⁶ Ibid.

¹⁸⁷ Ibid.

¹⁸⁸ Wikipedia, "Moses Malone," http://enwikipedia.org (accessed February 2013).

¹⁸⁹ "Lefty" Driesell, interviews (15–19 November 2012).

¹⁹⁰ Wikipedia, "Moses Malone," http://enwikipedia.org (accessed February 2013).

¹⁹¹ "Lefty" Driesell, interviews (15–19 November 2012).

¹⁹² Moses Malone, interview with the author by telephone (27 February 2013).

¹⁹³ Bolno, "Maryland Men's Basketball Digital Media Guide," 158.

¹⁹⁴ Ungrady, *Legends of Maryland Basketball,* 66–67; and McMullen, *Maryland Basketball: Tales from Cole Field House,* 84.

¹⁹⁵ "Lefty" Driesell, interviews (15–19 November 2012).

¹⁹⁶ Ibid.

¹⁹⁷ Ibid.

¹⁹⁸ Bolno, "Maryland Men's Basketball Digital Media Guide," 188–89.

¹⁹⁹ Wikipedia, "Albert King" and "Buck Williams," http://enwikipedia.org (accessed March 2013).

²⁰⁰ Bolno, "Maryland Men's Basketball Digital Media Guide," 189.

²⁰¹ McMullen, *Maryland Basketball: Tales from Cole Field House,* 83.

²⁰² Ibid., 85.

²⁰³ Curry Kirkpatrick, "Something's Gotta Give," *Sports Illustrated* (29 November 1982).

²⁰⁴ "Lefty" Driesell, interviews (15–19 November 2012).

²⁰⁵ Ungrady, *Legends of Maryland Basketball,* 79.

²⁰⁶ Ibid.

²⁰⁷ Ibid., 68.

²⁰⁸ Ibid., 69.

²⁰⁹ Ibid. Also, Holliday with Moore, *Hoop Tales: Maryland Terrapins Men's Basketball,* 89.

²¹⁰ McMullen, *Maryland Basketball: Tales from Cole Field House,* 92.

²¹¹ Ibid.

²¹² Ibid., 95.

213 Ibid. Also, Bolno, "Maryland Men's Basketball Digital Media Guide," 166.

214 Jon Cole, *The Citadel Bulldogs 2011–2012 Men's Basketball Media Guide* (Charleston SC: Citadel Printing and Copier Services, 2011) 30.

215 Ungrady, *Legends of Maryland Basketball,* 84; and McMullen, *Maryland Basketball: Tales from Cole Field House,* 106.

216 Ibid., 97.

217 Holliday with Moore, *Hoop Tales: Maryland Terrapins Men's Basketball,* 48.

218 Bomani Jones, "Len Bias Gone, but Not Forgotten," ESPN Page 2 (6 June 2006); and Holliday with Moore, *Hoop Tales: Maryland Terrapins Men's Basketball,* 55.

219 Frazier, "Without Bias," Michael Wilbon interview.

220 "Lefty" Driesell, interviews (15–19 November 2012); and Holliday with Moore, *Hoop Tales: Maryland Terrapins Men's Basketball,* 44–47.

221 Ibid.

222 Ibid., 48.

223 McMullen, *Maryland Basketball: Tales from Cole Field House,* 98.

224 Bolno, "Maryland Men's Basketball Digital Media Guide," 188; and McMullen, *Maryland Basketball: Tales from Cole Field House,* 98.

225 Ibid.

226 Ibid., 100.

227 Bolno, "Maryland Men's Basketball Digital Media Guide," 189.

228 Taylor, *2002–2003 Georgia State Basketball Fact Book,* 31.

229 McMullen, *Maryland Basketball: Tales from Cole Field House,* 101; Ungrady, *Legends of Maryland Basketball,* 73; and "Lefty" Driesell, interviews (15–19 November 2012).

230 Adrian Branch, interview with the author by telephone (5 March 2013).

231 Wikipedia, "Adrian Branch," http://enwikipedia.org (accessed March 2013).

232 Ungrady, *Legends of Maryland Basketball,* 86; and Bolno, "Maryland Men's Basketball Digital Media Guide," 165, 189.

233 Ungrady, *Legends of Maryland Basketball,* 86.

234 Ungrady, *Born Ready: The Mixed Legacy of Len Bias,* 60.

235 Ungrady, *Legends of Maryland Basketball,* 84–85.

236 Ibid.

237 Bolno, "Maryland Men's Basketball Digital Media Guide," 158, 166.

238 C. Fraser Smith, *Lenny, "Lefty" and the Chancellor,* 98–99.

[239] Ibid., 101–102; and Ungrady, *Legends of Maryland Basketball,* 86.

[240] "Lefty" Driesell, interviews (15–19 November 2012).

[241] Ibid.

[242] Ibid.

[243] Ibid.

[244] Ibid.

[245] Ibid.

[246] Ibid.

[247] Ibid.

[248] Joe Fitzgerald, "Well-Deserved Victory for 'Lefty,'" *Boston Herald* (28 August 1986).

[249] Evan Thomas, *The Man to See* (New York: Simon & Schuster, 1991) 462–63.

[250] "Lefty" Driesell, interviews (15–19 November 2012).

[251] Craig Neff and Bruce Selcraig, "One Shock Wave After Another," *Sports Illustrated* (10 November 1986); and Ungrady, *Born Ready: The Mixed Legacy of Len Bias,* 55.

[252] Ibid., 53–54.

[253] C. Fraser Smith, *Lenny, "Lefty," and the Chancellor,* 62–63, 204–205.

[254] Fraser Smith, "The Education of John Slaughter," *Regardie's* (March 1988) 136–37; Ungrady, *Born Ready: The Mixed Legacy of Len Bias,* 54; and C. Fraser Smith, *Lenny, "Lefty," and the Chancellor,* 216, 232–33.

[255] Ibid., 194.

[256] Ibid., 91, 198–99.

[257] Ungrady, *Born Ready: The Mixed Legacy of Len Bias,* 55.

[258] Ibid., 54–55.

[259] Ibid., 39. Also, "Lefty" Driesell, interviews (15–19 November 2012).

[260] Ibid.

[261] Ungrady, *Born Ready: The Mixed Legacy of Len Bias,* 56.

[262] Ibid. Also, "Lefty" Driesell, interviews (15–19 November 2012).

[263] Robert D. Novak, "'Lefty,' They Done You Wrong," *Washington Post* (2 November 1986); C. Fraser Smith, *Lenny, "Lefty," and the Chancellor,* 217, 220, 221; and *Webster's Seventh New Collegiate Dictionary* (Springfield MA: G. & C. Merriam Company, 1969) 768.

[264] Ungrady, *Born Ready: The Mixed Legacy of Len Bias,* 66; and C. Fraser Smith, *Lenny, "Lefty," and the Chancellor,* 276–78.

[265] David Davidson, "Inside Colleges," *Atlanta Journal/Constitution* (2 November 1986).

[266] C. Fraser Smith, *Lenny, "Lefty," and the Chancellor,* 203.

[267] Ibid., 217. Also, Ungrady, *Born Ready: The Mixed Legacy of Len Bias,* 55–56, 106–107.

[268] "Lefty" Driesell, memorandum to Dr. John Slaughter, members of the Board of Regents, members of task force on academic achievement (11 August 1986).

[269] "Lefty" Driesell, letter to Dr. John Slaughter (4 September 1986).

[270] "Lefty" Driesell, letter to Dr. John Slaughter (16 September 1986).

[271] Ungrady, *Born Ready: The Mixed Legacy of Len Bias,* 56.

[272] Fraser Smith, "The Education of John Slaughter," 143–44; and C. Fraser Smith, *Lenny, "Lefty," and the Chancellor,* 224.

[273] Ibid., 207–209; and "Lefty" Driesell, interviews (15–19 November 2012).

[274] Ibid.

[275] Ibid.

[276] Ibid. Also, Jim Schlosser, "Ex-ACC Coach Stars in New Game Plan," *Greensboro News & Record* (March 1987).

[277] Novak, "'Lefty,' They Done You Wrong," D8.

[278] Fraser Smith, "The Education of John Slaughter," 138–40; and John Slaughter, "Bringing Excellence to College Park," farewell remarks to Campus Senate as outgoing UM chancellor (1988); and Ungrady, *Born Ready: The Mixed Legacy of Len Bias,* 64–72.

[279] C. Fraser Smith, *Lenny, "Lefty," and the Chancellor,* 238; Maryland House of Delegates, resolution of congratulations to "Lefty" Driesell (2 March 1987); Maryland State Senate, resolution of congratulations to "Lefty" Driesell (2 March 1987); and University of Maryland Inter Fraternity Council, award of appreciation to "Lefty" Driesell, 1986.

[280] Ungrady, *Born Ready: The Mixed Legacy of Len Bias,* 60–61.

[281] Ibid.

[282] "Lefty" Driesell, interviews (15–19 November 2012).

[283] Schlosser, "Ex-ACC Coach Stars in New Game Plan," A1, A9.

[284] Ungrady, *Born Ready: The Mixed Legacy of Len Bias,* 67; and "Lefty" Driesell, interviews (15–19 November 2012).

[285] Wikipedia, "James Madison University," http://enwikipedia.org (accessed March 2013); and John A. Martin, Gary Michael, and Kevin Warner, *2012–2013 James Madison University Men's Basketball Media Guide* (Harrisonburg VA: JMU Multimedia Communications, 2012).

[286] Wikipedia, "Lou Campanelli," http://enwikipedia.org (accessed March 2013); Martin, Michael, and Warner, *2012–2013 James Madison University Men's Basketball Media Guide,* 89, 100.

[287] Russ Potts, interview with the author by telephone (29 March 2013).

[288] Ibid.

[289] Ibid.

[290] Jim Britt, interview with the author by telephone (2 April 2013).

[291] Martin, Michael, and Warner, *2012–2013 James Madison University Men's Basketball Media Guide,* 106–107, 119.

[292] Britt, interview (2 April 2013).

[293] Martin, Michael, and Warner, *2012–2013 James Madison University Men's Basketball Media Guide,* 101–103; and "Lefty" Driesell, interviews (15–19 November 2012).

[294] Martin, Michael, and Warner, *2012–2013 James Madison University Men's Basketball Media Guide,* 103; and Mike Hodge, "'Lefty' Announces Retirement Plan," *Harrisonburg Daily News Record* (March 1997).

[295] Ibid.

[296] Mike Hodge, "'Lefty' Deserved a Better Ending," *Harrisonburg Daily News Record* (20 March 1997).

[297] Ibid.

[298] "Lefty" Driesell, interviews (15–19 November 2012).

[299] Dustin Dopirak, "The Day that JMU Basketball Changed," *Harrisonburg Daily News Record* (October 2006).

[300] Potts, interview (29 March 2013).

[301] Martin Harmon, letter to Dr. Ronald Carrier (1 April 2013).

[302] Martin, Michael, and Warner, *2012–2013 James Madison University Men's Basketball Media Guide,* 103–104.

[303] "Lefty" Driesell, interviews (15–19 November 2012).

[304] Wikipedia, "Jim Harrick," enwikipedia.org (accessed April 2013).

[305] Martin, Michael, and Warner, *2012–2013 James Madison University Men's Basketball Media Guide,* 119; and "Lefty" Driesell, interviews (15–19 November 2012).

[306] Dave Cohen, interview with the author, Atlanta GA (11 April 2013).

[307] Taylor, *2002–2003 Georgia State Basketball Fact Book,* 166–71.

[308] Cohen, interview (11 April 2013).

[309] Ibid.

[310] Taylor, *2002–2003 Georgia State Basketball Fact Book,* 174.

[311] Cohen, interview (11 April 2013).

[312] "Lefty" Driesell, interviews (15–19 November 2012).

[313] Cohen, interview (11 April 2013).

[314] Ibid.

[315] Taylor, *2002–2003 Georgia State Basketball Factbook,* 174–76.

316 Cohen, interview (11 April 2013).

317 Taylor, *2002–2003 Georgia State Basketball Factbook,* 35.

318 Ibid., 145–51.

319 Cohen, interview (11 April 2013); and Taylor, *2002–2003 Georgia State Basketball Factbook,* 176.

320 Ibid. Also, Cohen, interview (11 April 2013).

321 Ibid.

322 Ibid.

323 Earnest Reese, "This Ain't No Mickey Mouse Team," *Atlanta Journal/Constitution* (12 March 2001).

324 Cohen, interview (11 April 2013).

325 Ibid. Also, Taylor, *2002–2003 Georgia State Basketball Factbook,* 176.

326 Ibid. Also, McMullen, *Maryland Basketball: Hoop Tales from Cole Field House,* 161–73.

327 Taylor, *2002–2003 Georgia State Basketball Factbook,* 176; Scott Fowler, "Final Curtain: Exit, Stage," *Charlotte Observer* (4 January 2003); and Ron Green, Sr., "'Lefty' Kept It Fun for a Long Time," *Charlotte Observer* (January 2003).

328 Cohen, interview (11 April 2013).

329 Michael Perry, interview with the author by telephone (22 April 2013).

330 Earnest Reese, "GSU Mourns for Teammate," *Atlanta Journal/Constitution* (1 November 2001); and Colin Martz, "Campus Stunned by Death of Teammate, Friend," *The GSU Signal* (6 November 2001).

331 Perry, interview (22 April 2013).

332 Tim Gayle, "Phil Cunningham Named Troy's Men's Basketball Coach," *Montgomery Advertiser* (26 March 2013); and Joshua Gleason, "Travis Williams's Difficult Route to Being Division I Head Coach," *Bleacher Report* (May 2013).

333 Wikipedia, "Gale Catlett," http://enwikipedia.org (accessed May 2013).

334 Joshua Gleason, "Travis Williams's Difficult Route to Being Division I Head Coach," *Bleacher Report* (May 2013).

335 Nicole Auerbach, "'Lefty' Driesell Not Pleased with Gary Williams Court Naming," *USA Today* (25 January 2012); and Jay Barker, "Maryland's 'Gary Williams Court' Result of Contentious Decision," *Baltimore Sun* (24 January 2012).

[336] Bolno, "Maryland Men's Basketball Digital Media Guide," 159; and Don Markus, "'Lefty' Driesell Honored with Bas-Relief at Comcast Center," *Baltimore Sun* (17 April 2013).

[337] Bob Cohn and David Elfin, "Driesell Not Invited to Cole Ceremonies," *Washington Times* (7 March 2002).

[338] Ibid.

[339] Bill Free, "Kehoe, Driesell: We Weren't Invited to Cole Farewell," *Baltimore Sun* (5 March 2002).

[340] Cohn and Elfin, "Driesell Not Invited to Cole Ceremonies," D1; and "Lefty" Driesell, interviews (15–19 November 2012).

[341] William E. Kirwan, letter to University of Maryland alumni and supporters (16 April 2013).

[342] Ron Green, Sr., "'Lefty' Kept It Fun for a Long Time," *Charlotte Observer* (January 2003).

[343] "Lefty" Driesell, interviews (15–19 November 2012).

[344] Ibid.

[345] Ibid.

[346] Carroll Rogers, "'Lefty' Driesell's Legacy Lives On in Daughter Pam, Son Chuck," *Atlanta Journal/Constitution* (29 November 2010); and "Lefty" Driesell, interviews (15–19 November 2012).

[347] Bob Colson, "50 from 50," *Sports Illustrated* (27 December 1999).

[348] Denise Kersten Wills, "45 Who Shaped Washington, 1965–2010," *Washingtonian* (October 2010).

[349] Judy Coffin, "The Professionals," *Charlotte Magazine* (July–August1977).

[350] "'Lefty' Driesell Defensive Player of the Year," and "'Lefty' Driesell Defensive All-America Team," CollegeInsider.com, http://collegeinsider.com (accessed May 2013); and "Stony Brook's Brenton Gets Driesell Award as Nation's Top Defender," *Baltimore Sun* (6 April 2013).

[351] Wikipedia, "'Lefty' Grove," http://enwikipedia.org (accessed April 2013).

[352] "Lefty" Driesell, interviews (15–19 November 2012).

Index

Due to the fact this biography contains a reference to Charles G. "Lefty" Driesell on virtually every page, he is not included in the index. Please be aware that along with "Lefty" (or simply Driesell), references to him also include "The Old Lefthander," another version of his familiar nickname respectfully conferred on him through the years by sportswriters, former assistant coaches, and other coaching colleagues, and understood by basketball fans ever since.

Index

Index

Index

Index